Achieving 'At-c

ANGLO-AMERIKANISCHE STUDIEN
ANGLO-AMERICAN STUDIES

Herausgegeben von Rüdiger Ahrens und Kevin Cope

Band 26

PETER LANG

Frankfurt am Main · Berlin · Bern · Bruxelles · New York · Oxford · Wien

Claudia Schemberg

Achieving 'At-one-ment'

Storytelling and the Concept of the *Self* in Ian McEwan's *The Child in Time*, *Black Dogs*, *Enduring Love*, and *Atonement*

PETER LANG
Europäischer Verlag der Wissenschaften

Bibliographic Information published by Die Deutsche Bibliothek
Die Deutsche Bibliothek lists this publication in the Deutsche Nationalbibliografie; detailed bibliographic data is available in the internet at <http://dnb.ddb.de>.

ISSN 0177-6959
ISBN 3-631-52782-9
US-ISBN 0-8204-7327-8

© Peter Lang GmbH
Europäischer Verlag der Wissenschaften
Frankfurt am Main 2004
All rights reserved.

All parts of this publication are protected by copyright. Any utilisation outside the strict limits of the copyright law, without the permission of the publisher, is forbidden and liable to prosecution. This applies in particular to reproductions, translations, microfilming, and storage and processing in electronic retrieval systems.

Printed in Germany 1 2 3 4 5 7

www.peterlang.de

Table of Contents

0.	INTRODUCTION	7
1.	THE STORIED *SELF* IN MORAL SPACE	11
	1.1 The Ethical Turn in Literary Criticism, or: Essays in Retrieval	11
	1.2 Facing Contingency: Fragmentations of *Self* and Morality	15
	1.3 Inescapable Frameworks and Shifting Horizons: Towards a Narrative Concept of the *Self*	19
2.	SETTING THE SCENE: THE POSTMODERN CHALLENGE TO THE *SELF*	25
	2.1 A Whole Supermarket of Theories: Exploring the Panorama of Ian McEwan's Novels	25
	2.2 Rising to the Challenge: Narrative (*Self-*)Creation	31
3.	UNFOLDING THE MAP OF LIFE: LOCATING THE *SELF*	39
	3.1 Being a *Self* to Yourself: Identity and Orientation	39
	3.2 *Self* Among Other *Selves*: Autonomy versus Commitment	43
4.	TAKING PERSPECTIVES: STORIES OF THE *SELF*	49
	4.1 The Poly-Storied *Self*: Selfhood and Cultural Tradition	49
	4.2 The Two Cultures Debate: Science versus Literature	51
	4.3 Metaphysician Meets Ironist: Rationalism, Scientism, and Mysticism	61
5.	AT THE CROSSROADS: THE IMPACT OF THE SINGULAR ON THE CONCEPT OF THE *SELF*	71
	5.1 Dealing with Epistemological Crises: Redescriptions and New Horizons	71
	5.2 Love, Loss, and Guilt: The Emotional Geography of the *Self*	81
6.	JOURNEY'S END: ACHIEVING 'AT-ONE-MENT'?	87
	6.1 Towards Greater Solidarity: Introducing the Liberal Ironist	87
	6.2 Tying Knots and Closing Questions?	91

| 7. | CONCLUSION | 97 |
| 8. | WORKS CITED | 101 |

0. Introduction

For over a decade Ian Russell McEwan found himself trapped in the role of the shocking sensationalist, caricatured by the British press as Ian Macabre, Ian Makesyouqueasy, and the Clapham Shocker.[1] The collections of short stories McEwan wrote at the beginning of his career, *First Love, Last Rites* (1975) and *In Between the Sheets, and Other Stories* (1978), as well as his first two novels *The Cement Garden* (1978) and *The Comfort of Strangers* (1981), were reviewed with an eye on the scatological, psychopathological, or pornographic. Isolating the "dirty" bits of his work, critics and scholars of the late 1970s and early 1980s either tended to condemn McEwan as obscene or praise him as liberated.[2] *The Child in Time* (1987) was the first of McEwan's novels not to achieve a *succèss de scandale*. It marked the beginning of the author's public transformation from an *enfant terrible* of the 1970s to one of the most revered "storytellers" of contemporary British culture. McEwan's examination of great philosophical concepts such as truth and reality, his prismatic exploration of the uncertainties and complexities of interpersonal relationships, and his critical but sympathetic study of human nature earned him a panoply of awards, including the 1998 Booker Prize for his novel *Amsterdam* (1998).

The Child in Time, *Black Dogs* (1992), *Enduring Love* (1997), and *Atonement* (2001) retain elements of the existential void, the "emotional and spiritual waste land of frustration [...], non-communication, isolation, and *la naussé*"[3] depicted in McEwan's early fiction. However, despite nightmarish episodes, McEwan's vision of the world in the four novels discussed in this paper is ultimately benign, distinguished by an optimism "to locate what is good"[4] in a universe of contingent forces. In his mature fiction, McEwan comes up with a philosophy that combines a respect for autonomous, free choice with a broad tolerance of heterogeneous world pictures and an imaginative engagement with the other. Though varying in their thematic scope, all four novels centre round the difficult yet inescapable task of searching for coherent structures of

---

[1] Brian Finney, "Briony's Stand Against Oblivion: Ian McEwan's *Atonement*," *Brian Finney's Website*, 2002, Dept. of English, California State University, 3 May 2003 <http://www.csulb.edu/~bhfinney/McEwan.html>. Cf. Dwight Garner, "The Salon Interview: Ian McEwan," *Salon.Com*, 31 Mar. 1998, 4 Feb. 2003 <http://dir.salon.com/books/int/ 1998/03/cov_si_31int.html>.
[2] Peter Lewis, "Ian McEwan," *Contemporary Novelists*, ed. D.L. Kirkpatrick (London: St. James, 1986) 591.
[3] Lewis, "Ian McEwan" 591.
[4] Jack Slay Jr., *Ian McEwan* (New York: Twayne; London: Prentice Hall, 1996) 148.

meaning and orientation in a (post)modern world characterised by a loss of horizon and the absence of ultimate Truth.

The yearning for coherent structures of meaning and orientation is deeply ingrained in human nature. In fact, as "pattern-building animals",[5] we are "unable to resist making sense of whatever data we encounter."[6] We continuously transform unstructured contingency into structured consistency, trying to answer pressing epistemological and ontological questions like "Who are we?", "Where are we?", and "Where are we going?"[7] We would like to argue in this paper that in times of epistemic crisis, nagging doubt, and fractured spirit we still strive for unity and wholeness in our lives, guided by a difficult to define and mostly tacit ideal of 'at-one-ment',[8] the feeling that our various choices and convictions should be tailored as far as possible to our individual needs, should indeed be 'at one' with what we perceive of as our unique *self*.[9]

Of all the tools of pattern-building that help us attain the unity and wholeness we strive for in our lives, language is the most effective.[10] In fact, we narratively construct and reconstruct our *selves* by telling coherent stories about who, where, and what we are and by comparing our accounts of the *self* with accounts of others. We are guided in our *self*-making activities by "presuppositions and perspectives about selfhood, rather like plot summaries or

---

[5] Heinz Antor, "Ethical Plurivocity, or: The Pleasures and Rewards of Reading," *Text – Culture – Reception. Cross- Cultural Aspects of English Studies*, ed. Rüdiger Ahrens and Heinz Antor (Heidelberg: C. Winter, 1992) 40.
[6] Wayne C. Booth, *The Company We Keep: An Ethics of Fiction* (Berkeley: University of California Press, 1988) 62.
[7] Cf. Heinz Antor, "The Ethics of Criticism in the Age After Value," *Why Literature Matters: Theories and Functions of Literature*, ed. Rüdiger Ahrens and Laurenz Volkmann (Heidelberg: C. Winter, 1996) 68.
[8] Ian McEwan coined the neologism 'at-one-ment' to refer to a "reconciliation with the *self*" (Kate Kellaway, "At Home with his Worries," *The Observer* 16 Sept. 2001, 10 Dec. 2002 <http://www.books.guardian...iction/story/0,6000,552557,00.html>). Kate Kellaway, summing up an interview she conducted with McEwan shortly after the publication of *Atonement*, states that McEwan was looking at the novel's title one day "when he saw, suddenly, how it came apart: at-one-ment" (Kellaway, "At Home").
[9] We use the term '(the) *self*' to refer to the individual human agent's sense of being an "I", a being of "depth and complexity" (Charles Taylor, *Sources of the Self. The Making of the Modern Identity*. Cambridge: Cambridge UP, 1989. 32) that cannot do without orientation to the good. From the point of view of philosophy, the concept of the *self*, or *soi*, or *Selbst* is "notoriously evasive to definition" (Jerome Bruner, *Making Stories: Law, Literature, Life*. New York: Farrar, 2002. 63) and often synonymously used with terms like person, agent, or subject. However, to point out the distinction between what is "I" and what is not "I", the dichotomy of "*self* and other" works better than that of, say, "person and other", or "agent and other". Moreover, as the term '(the) *self* is employed in the majority of theoretical texts quoted and referred to in this paper, we choose it for reasons of clarity and uniformity.
[10] Antor, "Ethics" 69.

homilies for telling oneself about oneself or others about oneself."[11] The sheer abundance of ways of life, the plurality and heterogeneity of stories of the *self* and the world provided by religion, philosophy, science, or mythology turn the art of (post)modern *self*-making into a challenge unprecedented in the history of Western culture.

In the last two decades, Anglo-American literary criticism has rediscovered fictional storytelling as an irreplaceable mode of rising to the challenge of (post)modern *self*-creation. After years of confusion and deconstructionist denial, scholars on both sides of the Atlantic are regaining confidence in literature's ability to provide undogmatic "guidance in an era bereft of foundations and facing confusing options, incommensurable values, and a mindless relativism."[12] From the late 1980s onwards, an increasing number of philosophers like Richard Rorty, Charles Taylor, and Alasdair MacIntyre and literary scholars such as Wayne C. Booth and Martha Nussbaum, have been expressing their dissatisfaction with the deconstructive dictum that "il n'y a pas de hors-texte",[13] i.e. that one cannot evaluate, criticise, or construe a meaning for a text by reference to anything external to it. While "ethical critics" like Rorty, Booth, and Taylor agree with deconstructive critics that there is no such thing as an unequivocal, single, or stable meaning, they reject the Derridean dogma of turning *différance*, i.e. the principle of "the continuous (and endless) postponement or deferral of meaning",[14] into an absolute. Ethical critics claim that in order to gain orientation in a world of uncharted diversity, human beings depend on structures of meaning. They hold that the pluriform discourse of literature constitutes an irreplaceable mode of acquainting us with a great number of meaningful ways of living "the good life."[15]

Ian McEwan's novels are characterised by a keen awareness of the important structuring and meaning-giving task that narrative in general and fictional storytelling in particular perform in our lives. In the following, we will try to incorporate the discussion of storytelling and the concept of the *self* in Ian McEwan's *The Child in Time, Black Dogs, Enduring Love,* and *Atonement* into the discourse of values revived by ethical critics in the 1980s and 1990s. We will not, however, submit McEwan's novels to an ethics test. Rather, we intend to focus on our encounter with McEwan's *ethos* or character, i.e. with his persisting characteristics as a storyteller.[16] We will analyse the various ways the

---

[11] Bruner, *Making Stories* 66.
[12] Vernon W. Gras, "The Recent Ethical Turn in Literary Studies," *Mitteilungen des Verbandes Deutscher Anglisten* 4.2 (1993): 30.
[13] Jacques Derrida (*Of Grammatology*) quoted in J.A. Cuddon, *The Penguin Dictionary of Literary Terms and Literary Theory*, 3rd ed. (London: Penguin, 1992) 225.
[14] Cuddon, *Dictionary* 224.
[15] Taylor, *Sources* 3.
[16] Booth, *Company* 8.

characters and narrators in the four novels structure their world, endow it with meaning, and strive for 'at-one-ment' in their lives.

Chapter one constitutes the theoretical backbone of the ensuing discussion. It emphasises the salient role of ethical criticism in the domain of literary studies at the turn of the millennium, traces the roots of the fragmentation of the *self* and of morality observed in today's liberal societies, and introduces a narrative concept of the *self* that acknowledges our universal need for structures of meaning and orientation, while taking into account the plurality and heterogeneity of (post)modern ways of life. Chapter two offers an overview of the postmodern panorama of Ian McEwan's novels. It briefly places them in the context of contemporary British literature and concludes with an analysis of the connection between narrative (*self-*)creation and the creation of meaning in the four novels. Chapter three focusses on the concept of the *self* implicit in the discussion of narrative (*self-*)creation, elucidating the interplay between *self* and other, autonomy and commitment that characterises the protagonists' social world. In chapter four, we argue that as *selves* we are not only immersed in a community with living members of our respective societies, but find ourselves part of a particular cultural history. We discuss the characters' adherence to stories of the *self* and the world furnished by science, literature, and religion. Chapter five centres on the premise that in (post)modern times none of the explanatory patterns examined in chapter four can claim universal validity and secure us permanently against the impact of contingency. We follow the paths of the characters as they negotiate epistemological crises and round off our discussion with a cognitive-evaluative appraisal of emotions such as grief, love, loss, and guilt. The final chapter of this paper turns yet again to the interplay of the social and the private in Ian McEwan's novels, positing that individual *self*-creation does not perforce run counter to the ideal of human solidarity.

1. The Storied *Self* in Moral Space

1.1 The Ethical Turn in Literary Criticism, or: Essays in Retrieval

Storytelling is a mode of "world-making"[17] unique to the human species, facilitated by an evolutionary increase in hominid brain size, the development of an innate language faculty, and a mimetic sense that empowered early man "to re-enact or imitate events in the present or past."[18] In the course of human history, the social practice of storytelling proved an indispensable vehicle for "passing on a culture's ways"[19] and became a useful means of educating people into the moral values of their respective societies. In Western culture, the link between ethics and aesthetics dates back to Antiquity and the portrayal of heroic virtues in the Sagas of the Norsemen and the Homeric poems of ancient Greece.[20] The moral conflicts staged in Sophoclean tragedy, the descriptions of the ideal polis in Plato's *Republic*, and Aristotle's account of the virtues in his *Nicomachean Ethics*, are instances of a budding literary-ethical tradition that continued to flourish in the Christian Middle Ages, throughout the Renaissance, and well into the seventeenth century.[21] With the founding of academic history in the late seventeenth century, "morality" was allowed a cultural space of its own and the ties binding the ethical to the aesthetic began to loosen.[22] When ethical norms and textual meaning gave way to the free play of *différance* in the literary movements of deconstruction and post-structuralism in the 1960s and 1970s, approaching literature from an ethical point of view was dismissed as "affective fallacy"[23] and the old ties between literature and ethics were severed in what seemed like a final *coup de grâce*.

However harshly assaulted by deconstructive and post-structuralist theory, in practice ethical criticism refused to die.[24] Readers went on evaluating literature, stories continued to matter to them, providing practical guidance, comfort, entertainment, or yielding some other carry-over into the non-literary world. For the reader untouched by deconstructive thinking, art remained very much tied to life. In the late 1980s and early 1990s, a growing number of

---

[17] Peter Lamarque and Olson Haugom Stein, *Truth, Fiction and Literature* (Oxford: Clarendon, 1994) 37.
[18] Bruner, *Making Stories* 96. For a book-length study on the nature of human language refer to: Noam Chomsky, *Knowledge of Language: Its Nature, Origin and Use* (New York: Praeger, 1986).
[19] Bruner, *Making Stories* 96.
[20] MacIntyre, *AfterVirtue* (1981; London: Duckworth, 1985) 114ff. Cf. Antor, "Ethics" 65f.
[21] MacIntyre, *After Virtue* 123ff.
[22] MacIntyre, *After Virtue* 38.
[23] Booth, *Company* 4.
[24] Booth, *Company* 6.

scholars began to deplore "the exile of evaluation"[25] within the literary academy, complaining like Martha Nussbaum about "the absence, from literary theory, of the organizing questions of moral philosophy."[26] The theories advanced by literary scholars like Wayne C. Booth, J. Hillis Miller, Barbara Herrnstein Smith, and Martha Nussbaum, and by contemporary philosophers like Richard Rorty, Charles Taylor, and Alasdair MacIntyre, to name but a few, helped prepare an "ethical turn"[27] in Anglo-American literary studies that brought new life to the ancient discourse of values and continues "to exert a positive influence on the subject of literary studies [...]."[28]

Why return to ethics in the age of postmodernism,[29] where prescriptive teleologies and universalisms have been left behind, where we have shrugged off what Jean-François Lyotard called the *grand récits*[30] of our ancestors, and are prepared to face contingency unflinchingly? It seems, after all, that ethical questions are inescapable. Even the most forbidding censors of an ethical approach to literature who tried "to purge themselves of all but the most abstract formal interests turn out to have an ethical program in mind – a belief that a given way of reading, or a given kind of literature will do us most good."[31] Despite their formal rejection of evaluation, deconstructive approaches to literature are laden with value, "since every negative evaluation, even of the practice of evaluation itself, must always constitute a kind of evaluation on its

---

[25] Barbara Herrnstein Smith, *Contingencies of Value. Alternative Perspectives for Critical Theory* (Cambridge, Mass.: Harvard UP, 1988) 17.
[26] Martha C. Nussbaum, "Perceptive Equilibrium: Literary Theory and Ethical Theory," *The Future of Literary Theory*, ed. Ralph Cohen (London: Routledge, 1989) 60.
[27] Gras, "Ethical Turn" 30.
[28] Antor, "Ethics" 65.
[29] The term 'postmodernism' was first employed by the German philosopher Rudolf Pannwitz in *Die Krisis der Europäischen Kultur* (1917) to describe the Nietzschean 'nihilism' of twentieth-century Western culture. The term only came into expanded use in the 1970s with influential works like Charles Jenck's *The Language of Postmodern Architecture* (1977), Jean François Lyotard's *La condition postmoderne: rapport sur le savoir* (1979), or Richard Rorty's *Philosophy and the Mirror of Nature* (1979). Lawrence Cahoone, ed., Introduction, *From Modernism to Postmodernism. An Anthology* (1996; Oxford: Blackwell, 2000) 3ff and Linda Hutcheon, *The Politics of Postmodernism* (London: Routledge, 1989) 11ff.
[30] Lyotard coined the term '*grand récit*' in *La condition postmoderne* (1979) to criticise the great ideologies, or *grand récits* (master narratives), put forward by religion, science, and Enlightenment philosophy. See: Anton Hügli and Poul Lübcke, *Philosophielexikon. Personen und Begriffe der abendländischen Philosophie von der Antike bis zur Gegenwart* (1991; Hamburg: Rowohlt, 2001) 403f. Cf. Wolfgang Welsch, *Unsere Postmoderne Moderne* (Berlin: Akademischer Verlag, 1997) 31ff.
[31] Booth, *Company* 5. Cf. Richard Freadman and Seumas Miller, *Re-Thinking Theory: A Critique of Contemporary Literary Theory and an Alternative Account* (Cambridge: Cambridge UP, 1992) 70.

own terms, even if it implies or states no positive alternative value."[32] Throughout our lives we estimate, ascribe, modify, affirm, or deny value, we embrace ideas and reject others, we make decisions or decide not to decide. As Charles Taylor puts it, "being a self is inseparable from existing in a space of moral issues, to do with identity and how one ought to be. It is being able to find one's standpoint in this space, being able to occupy, to be a perspective in it."[33] Since we cannot approach literature in the neutral, value-free way that deconstructive thinkers had in mind, why not invite ethical criticism back into the front parlour of literary discourse and see if it does provide answers to the Aristotelian question "How should one live?"[34]

Literature is much more than a handmaiden of contemporary moral philosophy; in fact, it is especially well-suited to deal with questions concerning the good life. Iris Murdoch observed as early as 1961 that

> we require [...] a renewed sense of the difficulty and complexity of the moral life and the opacity of persons. We need more concepts in terms of which to picture the substance of our being. [...] Through literature we can re-discover a sense of the density of our lives.[35]

If we dare to look beyond traditional philosophy, if we wish to discover further concepts which we can use to illustrate a "complete human life lived at its best",[36] we need to turn to such texts as novels, "texts engaged in the shaping of the language of particularity."[37] While philosophy is traditionally characterised by a "pitchfork mentality"[38] that deals in moral theses and values orderly lines of argumentation leading to conclusions that transcend the particular, literature is concerned with the circumstantial or singular aspects of moral living. It puts forward hypotheses and reaches only "provisional conclusion[s] in which nothing is concluded, implying the continuation of moral reassessment, surprise, doubt, mental travelling, musing."[39] Thus, literature compellingly portrays the

---

[32] Steven Connor, *Theory and Cultural Value* (1988; London: Blackwell, 1992) 15.

[33] Taylor, *Sources* 112.

[34] Nussbaum, "Perceptive Equilibrium" 63.

[35] Quoted in Jane Adamson, "Against Tidiness. Literature and/versus Moral Philosophy," *Renegotiating Ethics in Literature, Philosophy, and Theory*, ed. Jane Adamson, Richard Freadman, and David Parker (Cambridge: Cambridge UP, 1998) 85.

[36] MacIntyre, *After Virtue* 140.

[37] Cora Diamond, "Martha Nussbaum and the Need for Novels," *Renegotiating Ethics in Literature, Philosophy, and Theory*, ed. Jane Adamson, Richard Freadman, and David Parker (Cambridge: Cambridge UP, 1998) 64.

[38] Adamson, "Against Tidiness" 102.

[39] Adamson, "Against Tidiness" 104. Note, however, that there exists a rich literary tradition that puts forward firm moral convictions. Novels written in the third person "omniscient" voice of the nineteenth century are an example of this overtly didactic kind of literature with a palpable moral design.

ambiguity and complexity of a world where we must take a stand, where "positionality"[40] is required of us, where we must choose between conflicting values, yet where no single perspective can claim universal validity. As Vernon C. Gras points out with reference to our postmodern condition, "the struggle that accompanies choice is far more effectively shown in literary narrative than in philosophy."[41]

However, in order to develop new concepts in terms of which to picture the substance of our being, literary criticism needs philosophy's clear-cut "vocabulary of moral and political reflection",[42] its centuries-old expertise in seeking, scrutinising, and analysing structures of human experience. The difficult task of placing ourselves in a complex world of conflicting choices is alleviated by the possession of a vocabulary in which to phrase those choices and thus map the *terra incognita* lying ahead of us. Still, we should remember that there is no vocabulary or process of pattern-building that insulates us permanently against the contingency of a universe in which a confusing number of conflicting concepts is abroad.[43] The pluriform discourse of literature reminds us of the density of our lives and of the provisionality of all patterns of meaning. It acquaints us with new possible modes of living a good life, and entices us to reweave "our vocabulary of moral deliberation to accommodate new beliefs."[44] In fact, literature and philosophy are different modes of inquiry into the nature of human experience. They complement each other, showing different facets of what it means for us to exist in a space of moral issues, or, as Alasdair MacIntyre puts it, what it means to be a "moral agent."[45] Prolific ethical criticism retrieves the scrutinising and analysing techniques perfected in centuries of moral philosophy and turns to literature to learn to read with a different sort of eye, "coming to realise what Martha Nussbaum aptly calls 'the complexity, the indeterminacy, the sheer difficulty' of actual moral experience."[46]

Implicit in our discussion so far, has been the claim that we need a literary discourse that goes further than the ideological demystification or deconstruction of totalising teleologies undertaken by deconstructive or post-structuralist criticism.[47] We need a discourse that puts us back in touch with the

---

[40] Antor, "Ethics" 70.
[41] Gras, "Ethical Turn" 38.
[42] Richard Rorty, *Contingency, Irony and Solidarity* (Cambridge: Cambridge UP, 1989) 44.
[43] Rorty, *Contingency* 7ff.
[44] Rorty, *Contingency* 196.
[45] MacIntyre, *After Virtue* 30.
[46] Adamson, "Against Tidiness" 98, cf. Andrew Gibson, *Postmodernity, Ethics and the Novel* (London: Routledge, 1999) 7f.
[47] David Parker, "The Turn to Ethics in the 1990s," Introduction, *Renegotiating Ethics in Literature, Philosophy, and Theory*, ed. Jane Adamson, Richard Freadman, and David Parker (Cambridge: Cambridge UP, 1998) 7.

ethical dimension of literary texts and offers us pragmatic solutions to the difficult (moral) choices we are faced with in life. As Gras points out, "[t]he weakness of deconstruction is that once it had achieved its aim – reiterating the non-presence of Presence, the loss of the center, the impossibility of jumping the culture /'nature' gap – it had little to offer in the everyday world of concrete choices."[48] Ethical criticism as practised by Wayne C. Booth, Richard Rorty, Martha Nussbaum, Charles Taylor, and others undertakes to leave the ivory tower of an abstract aesthetic criticism out of touch with everyday experience; it goes in search of a pragmatic *ethos* that offers us some conceptual toeholds,[49] but nevertheless acknowledges the plurality of postmodern life-choices and avoids falling into the trap of metaphysical illusions. In other words, we are in favour of a post-post-structuralist literary criticism which acknowledges more openly "the latent metaphysical dependencies of the critical attempt to suppress value, without giving up on the gains which that critical move has brought us."[50]

We will try and come up with what Richard Rorty calls an "antirepresentationalist account", i.e. an account that is not concerned with getting reality right, but rather strives to acquaint us with "habits of action for coping with reality."[51] Successful ethical criticism thus understood will have to perform a careful balancing act steering past "the Scylla of old-fashioned essentialism and the Charybdis of a new-fangled arbitrary valuelessness in which anything goes."[52] It will integrate into its theories the lessons that (post)modernism has rightfully taught us about the plurality of world-views, the contingency of truth, and the pitfalls of prescriptive teleologies, yet at the same time reincorporate some of the cultural inheritance we have carried around with us ever since Antiquity. In the process, a concept of the *self* will be developed that takes into account our basic need for meaningful patterns and *teloi* exemplified in centuries of storytelling and philosophy, yet is tailored for the special circumstance of being at home in liberal Western societies at the beginning of a new millennium.

1.2   Facing Contingency: Fragmentations of *Self* and Morality

Any concept of the *self* and of morality is rooted in the present as well as in the past of the cultural community in which it is formulated. As Alasdair

---

[48] Gras, "Ethical Turn" 35.
[49] Richard Rorty, *Objectivity, Relativism, and Truth* (Cambridge: Cambridge UP, 1991) 14.
[50] Kate Soper, "Postmodernism, Subjectivity and the Question of Value," *Principled Positions: Postmodernism and the Rediscovery of Value*, ed. J. Squires (London: Lawrence & Wishart, 1993) 28.
[51] Rorty, *Objectivity* 1.
[52] Antor, "Ethics" 66f.

MacIntyre points out, "the history of our [...] lives is generally and characteristically embedded in and made intelligible in terms of the larger and longer histories of a number of traditions."[53] Similarly, Charles Taylor argues that our culture has gradually transformed over the centuries into what it is now and that "we cannot understand ourselves without coming to grips with this history."[54] Postmodernism, however, often "takes on an oppositional, confrontational, and negative rhetoric against the past",[55] challenging "the entire notion of continuity in history and its writing."[56] In our post-metaphysical culture, telic patterns of explanation implicating "the discovery of the universal conditions of human existence, the great continuities – the permanent, ahistorical, context of human life",[57] have given way to the recognition of the individuality, heterogeneity, and contingency of human existence. In the post-Darwinian accounts of our time, human culture is no longer uniformly progressing towards a purpose designed by God or Nature, but "a result of thousands of small mutations finding niches [...]."[58] The grand totalising narratives of our metaphysical past have been replaced by an array of smaller, fragmentary, or conflicting local narratives that cannot claim objective, universal validity. Charles Taylor draws our attention to the "essentially modern predicament"[59] inherent in the uncertain nature of moral commitments. He holds that the controversies about moral beliefs and the uncertainty regarding all convictions leave us groping helplessly for meaning in our lives and may tempt us to convert to an "anything goes" mentality that suppresses all moral ontology.[60] MacIntyre, in a similar way, deplores the postmodern tendency to regard evaluative utterances as mere expressions of personal feeling. He claims that "we have - very largely, if not entirely - lost our comprehension, both theoretically and practically, of morality"[61] and are left to grapple blindly with moral fragments that were once at home in greater telic narratives.

According to MacIntyre, the fragmentation of morality apparent in today's liberal societies dates back to the failure of what he calls "the Enlightenment project."[62] In the Enlightenment, the Platonic and Judeo-Christian concept of man endowed with "an essential nature and an essential purpose or function",[63] a True *Self* aspiring to True Eternal Reality, gave way to

---

[53] MacIntyre, *After Virtue* 207.
[54] Taylor, *Sources* ix.
[55] Gras, "Ethical Turn" 31.
[56] Hutcheon, *Politics* 65.
[57] Rorty, *Contingency* 26.
[58] Rorty, *Contingency* 16.
[59] Taylor, *Sources* 10.
[60] Taylor, *Sources* 10f.
[61] MacIntyre, *After Virtue* 2.
[62] MacIntyre, *After Virtue* 35.
[63] MacIntyre, *After Virtue* 56.

the ideal of the autonomous, rational individual liberated from his[64] imprisonment within "a theistic and teleological world order."[65] Philosophers as different as Diderot, Hume, Locke, Bentham, and Kant set out to replace what they took to be discredited traditional and superstitious forms of morality by secular versions of morality.[66] Rorty observes that in the course of the seventeenth and eighteenth centuries, the True *Self* of Platonism and Christianity was replaced by the notion of a True Inner *Self* or the God within. Thus, "the attempt to escape from the world of time and chance"[67] was shifted from the world hereafter to the essential human nature inside each of us. Like the Greek philosophers before them, the rationalist philosophers of the Enlightenment and the German Idealists of the eighteenth and nineteenth century "tried to formulate moral principles to which no adequately reflective [...] person could refuse allegiance."[68] It turned out, however, that with the birth of the modern, autonomous *self* and the falling away of a universally accepted *telos* in relation to which particular moral judgements could be safely evaluated as true or false, reaching an enduring agreement about moral principles represented an impossible task. All that philosophers ever came up with were sets of "mutually antagonistic moral stances, each claiming to have achieved [...] rational justification, but each also disputing this claim on the part of its rivals."[69]

It was Nietzsche who first circumvented the problem of arriving at universally accepted moral principles by dropping the whole idea of knowing the Truth in a clear, direct, and intersubjective form and by giving up "the idea of finding a single context for all human lives."[70] Today, we are aware of the fact that neither the world nor the *self* have an intrinsic or divine nature, that we are not "born equipped with an invariant, timeless self, a kind of secular equivalent of the soul",[71] and that there exists no such thing as the Cartesian *cogito* that rationally reasons its way to some monolithic Truth. However,

---

[64] For 'his' read 'his or her', for 'he' read 'he or she', for 'him' read 'him or her', for 'man' read 'man or woman', here, and in all ensuing cases.

[65] MacIntyre, *After Virtue* 58.

[66] MacIntyre, *After Virtue* 35ff.

[67] Rorty, *Objectivity*, 118.

[68] Alasdair MacIntyre, "The Claims of After Virtue," *The MacIntyre Reader*, ed. Kevin Knight (Cambridge: Polity, 1998) 70. Rorty points out that even Romanticism, which turned away from Enlightenment philosophy by marking the cult of feeling over pure rationality, held fast to the "enlightened" notion that there is "something common to all men at all times, not just one man once" (Rorty, *Contingency* 25).

[69] Rorty, *Contingency* 70.

[70] Rorty, *Contingency* 27. Cf. Lothar Bredella, "Aesthetics and Ethics: Incommensurable, Identical or Conflicting?" *Ethics and Aesthetics: The Moral Turn of Postmodernism*, ed. Gerhard Hoffmann and Alfred Hornung (Heidelberg: C. Winter, 1996) 32.

[71] Paul John Eakin, *How Our Lives Become Stories: Making Selves* (Ithaka, London: Cornell UP, 1999) 20.

abandoning the notion of universalisability and renouncing the belief in a quasi-divine *self*, did not put an end to confusion. By doing away with the universalisability of moral positions and the homogeneity of selfhood, Western culture suffered a loss of horizon[72] and selfhood became a hazy concept "intuitively obvious to common sense, yet notoriously evasive to definition [...]."[73]

A common reaction to the difficulty of moral deliberation and the formulation of coherent concepts of selfhood is illustrated in the attitude of what MacIntyre calls the "emotivist character."[74] The emotivist character subscribes to "the doctrine that all evaluative judgements, and more specifically all moral judgements, are *nothing but* expressions of preference, expressions of attitude or feeling, insofar as they are moral or evaluative in character."[75] Lacking any ultimate criteria of evaluation, the emotivist character drifts arbitrarily from one moral commitment to another. Cut off from stable social definitions and firm principles of value, he possesses "no given continuities, save those of the body [...] and of the memory which to the best of its ability gathers in the past."[76] The fragmented character of emotivist culture denies the legitimacy of traditional telic narratives and rational thinking, conceiving of himself as a self-sufficient, autonomous moral subject in the sense of the Nietzschean *Übermensch*.

In literary theory, emotivist culture helped engender the decentred, split subject of post-structuralist and deconstructive theory, i.e. a subject no longer regarded as a unified entity or a coherent *self*, but unmasked as a "discursive construction",[77] a "fictional product of groundless social narrative."[78] Convinced that all attempts at controlling language are expressions of the will to power[79] or, at best, illusionary, Roland Barthes declared the death of the author, "denouncing the holistic view of a self-determining, isolable, and independent 'Author-God' as 'the epitome and culmination of capitalist ideology.' "[80] Similarly, Michel Foucault struggles to "eliminate the constitutive subject", wishing to "end the reign of terror that he associates with the human history by turning to language as the only ethical subject."[81] The project of deconstruction, driven by the wish to unmask naïve hermeneutic understanding and shatter

---

[72] Taylor, *Sources* 17.
[73] Bruner, *Making Stories* 63.
[74] MacIntyre, *After Virtue* 26.
[75] MacIntyre, *After Virtue* 11.
[76] MacIntyre, *After Virtue* 31.
[77] Freadman and Miller, *Re-Thinking* 58.
[78] Freadman and Miller, *Re-Thinking* 62.
[79] See Michel Foucault, *The History of Sexuality: An Introduction*, trans. Robert Hurley, vol. 1 (London: Penguin, 1978) 133ff and Michel Foucault, *The History of Sexuality: The Use of Pleasure*, trans. Robert Hurley, vol. 2 (1984; London: Penguin, 1992) 171ff.
[80] Antor, "Ethical Plurivocity" 28.
[81] Tobin Siebers, *The Ethics of Criticism* (Ithaca: Cornell UP, 1988) 3.

bourgeois complacency, tries to persuade us to obey unconditionally "an ominous law which condemns us to deconstruct texts"[82] and repudiates the notion of moral agency. However, as Lothar Bredella points out, we pay a high price for deconstructive reading.[83] Literary texts that have become "unreadable" might prevent us from getting ensnared by bourgeois ideology, but at the same time fail to help us come to terms with the world we live in, i.e. fail to provide pragmatic answers to the question we cannot avoid asking ourselves: "How should one live?"

1.3 Inescapable Frameworks and Shifting Horizons: Towards a Narrative Concept of the *Self*

Substituting discursive construction for a coherent concept of the *self* turns out to be "a premature burial."[84] Just as evaluation cannot be exiled from our lives, the notion of possessing a coherent *self*, some stable, fixed, unchallengeable core of identity that marks us as uniquely "I"[85] in opposition to outward other, remains unquestioned in everyday life. Our modern concept of the *self*, our very notion of what it means to be a human agent, is founded on a "sense of inwardness"[86] and individuality persistent even in the face of neurobiological evidence which reduces our substantial concept of the *self* to haphazard "stimulus inputs to different parts of the brain."[87] Charles Taylor voices a common belief when he claims that "we naturally think that we have selves the way we have heads or arms, and inner depth the way we have hearts or livers, as a matter of hard, interpretation-free fact."[88]

---

[82] Bredella, "Aesthetics" 44.
[83] Christopher Cordner, "F.R. Leavis and the Moral in Literature," *On Literary Theory and Philosophy: A Cross-Disciplinary Encounter*, ed. Richard Freadman and Lloyd Reinhardt (London: Macmillan, 1991) 44.
[84] Siebers, *Ethics of Criticism* 4.
[85] Donald Davidson states that the use of the first person pronoun 'I' - and indeed of all other first person pronouns - constitutes an irreplaceable and irreducible way of positioning our*selves* with relation to places, objects, times, and people in everyday life, whereas "the phrase 'the self' doesn't play any clear role in ordinary speech" (Donald Davidson, *Subjective, Intersubjective, Objective*. Oxford: Oxford UP, 2001. 86).
[86] Taylor, *Sources* ix.
[87] Eakin, *How Our Lives Become Stories* 15. In a discussion about the complexity of the brain's capacities, neurobiologist and Nobel-laureate Gerald M. Edelman explained that the human cerebral cortex contains "ten billion neurons, at least – and a million billion connections. If you counted the connections, one per second, you'd finish counting them all thirty-two million years" (Eakin, *How Our Lives Become Stories* 13). Thus, from the point of view of neurobiology, there is almost no end to *self*-creation.
[88] Taylor, *Sources* 112.

Richard Rorty points out that "there is no harm in continuing to speak of a distinct entity called 'the self' which consists of the mental states of the human being: her beliefs, desires, moods, etc."[89] He stresses, however, that it is important to look upon the collection of those mental states "as *being* the self rather than something which the self *has*."[90] Thus, the *self* does not *have* an irreducible, impervious, and unchanging central core, but *is* a "substantial and 'continually developing' permeable coalescence of affection and reflection, of 'attachments' and desires"[91] which we, despite its heterogeneity, experience as unity. If the *self* is a conglomeration of mental states as changeable and diverse as beliefs, desires, moods, and emotions, how does it gain the unity we ascribe to it? Charles Taylor posits that our notion of the unity of selfhood "is bound up with and depends on what one can call [the] 'moral topography' "[92] of our lives. This moral topography is demarcated by specific frameworks of belief "which articulate our sense of orientation in the space of questions about the good."[93] Living within qualitative horizons which define these frameworks "is constitutive of human agency [and] stepping outside these limits would be tantamount to stepping outside what we would recognise as integral, that is, undamaged human personhood."[94] Hence, frameworks of belief are inescapable, they provide the only means of orientation in a complex and many-tiered universe in which we must take a stand. Throughout our lives, we search for best accounts,[95] i.e. frameworks of belief that reliably guide our choices and reactions in singular instances, make best sense of our individual existence, and offer conceptual toeholds that keep our lives from falling into arbitrariness.

Given the complexity and diversity of possible ways of modern life, we must rank the goods on offer by contrasting them or grading them hierarchically; putting, for example, the love of our family before independence, or the love of God before any other good.[96] As Taylor puts it,

---

[89] Rorty, *Objectivity* 123.
[90] Rorty, *Objectivity* 123.
[91] Simon Haines, "Deepening the Self. The Language of Ethics and the Language of Literature," *Renegotiating Ethics in Literature, Philosophy, and Theory*, ed. Jane Adamson, Richard Freadman, and David Parker (Cambridge: Cambridge UP, 1998) 35.
[92] Taylor, *Sources* 106.
[93] Taylor, *Sources* 41.
[94] Taylor, *Sources* 27.
[95] Taylor, *Sources* 58.
[96] Taylor, *Sources* 62. Note that by 'good', we understand "anything considered valuable, worthy, admirable, of whatever kind or category" (Taylor, *Sources* 92) by people in their individual lives.

even if we are not single-mindedly committed to one good we all have hypergoods which are not only incomparably more important than others, but provide the standpoint from which the other goods must be weighed, judged, decided about.[97]

Turning towards a private hypergood, or *teleion agathon* ('supreme good'), gives us a sense of wholeness and fullness of the *self*, just as moving away from it "strikes at the very roots"[98] of our identity. Thus, although no framework of belief can claim universal acceptance as an unchallengeable, objective fact, we still can - and indeed must, if we do not want to lose our sense of coherent selfhood - "make admirable sense of our lives even if we cease to have [...] an 'ambition of transcendence.' "[99]

Selfhood, however, is never a purely private event. Unlike Nietzsche, whose *Übermensch* transcends the social world and finds the good only in himself, Taylor subscribes to the Aristotelian concept of man as *zoon politicon*, claiming that "one is a self only among other selves. A self can never be described without reference to those that surround it."[100] We exist, Taylor proceeds, "in webs of interlocution",[101] deriving our *self*-definition from the interchange with other *selves*, or interlocutors, whose ideas, beliefs, and attachments we encounter in the present as well as in the past, in direct conversation as well as in the form of written record. Similarly, Mikhail Bakhtin's dialogism posits that we are no "self-contained monads, but [...] constituted through the relation of alterity between self (the 'I-in-me') and Other (the 'not-I-in-me'), as it occurs within the concrete life-world."[102] Seyla Benhabib's discourse ethics is likewise based on the assumption that we are *selves* in community with other *selves*, and that, for lack of a universally accepted master version of the *self*, we need to "practice the reversibility of standpoints"[103] in open-ended, ongoing moral conversations. Benhabib's "enlarged mentality"[104] or Rorty's "growth of minds"[105] can only be achieved if we are willing to shift our habitual horizons from time to time, if we are prepared to formulate "passing theories"[106] that are open to correction and allow for change. As Rorty puts it, all we can do in a universe devoid of preconceived

---

[97] Taylor, *Sources* 63 and 66.
[98] Taylor, *Sources* 63.
[99] Rorty, *Objectivity* 12.
[100] Taylor, *Sources* 35. Cf. MacIntyre, *After Virtue* 239.
[101] Taylor, *Sources* 36.
[102] Michael Gardiner, "Alterity and Ethics: A Dialogical Perspective," *Theory, Culture and Society* 13 (1996): 134.
[103] Seyla Benhabib, *Situating the Self: Gender, Community and Postmodernism in Contemporary Ethics* (Cambridge: Cambridge UP, 1992) 52.
[104] Benhabib, *Situating* 9.
[105] Rorty, *Objectivity* 14.
[106] Rorty, *Contingency* 14.

meaning is reweave our webs of belief[107] or, in Taylor's words, to change "webs of interlocution" and the nature of our dependence, yet without ever severing our dependence on those webs as a whole.[108]

Jerome Bruner, following in the wake of Rorty and Taylor, points out that "we constantly construct and reconstruct our selves to meet the needs of the situations we encounter"[109] and that this continuous process of "self-making is a narrative art."[110] Heinz Antor likewise asserts that

> [m]ost of us [...] think of our lives and of what constitutes the good life for us in terms of narrative structure, and as children and even in adult life we are socialized and educated into the virtues through the telling of stories.[111]

Selfhood, as Bruner puts it, is a "verbalized event [...], a kind of meta-event that gives coherence and continuity to the scramble of experience"[112] encountered in a world with no intrinsic structures. The unity of the *self* that we experience in our lives is hence not achieved by the mere possession of frameworks of belief, but by the articulation and integration of those frameworks into the greater stories of our lives. Once equipped with the capacity to narrate,[113] "we can produce a selfhood that joins us with others, that permits us to hark back selectively to our past while shaping ourselves for the possibilities of an imagined future."[114]

While the prescriptive master narratives of our metaphysical past imposed an "ontological hardening on our various versions of the real world"[115] and produced a selfhood that was rigidly mapped out in its future possibilities, post-metaphysical *self*-narrative leaves room for individual choice. MacIntyre posits that modern *self*-making is a "quest" whose *telos* is not universally impressed on us with birth, but individually created and recreated in the course of our lives.[116] Modern *self*-narrative is a balancing act between a certain autonomy, a degree of choice and possibility, and a dependence on "a world of others – [...] friends

---

[107] Rorty, *Objectivity* 101.
[108] Taylor, *Sources* 39.
[109] Bruner, *Making Stories* 64.
[110] Bruner, *Making Stories* 65.
[111] Antor, "Ethics" 66.
[112] Bruner, *Making Stories* 73.
[113] The capacity to narrate is an evolutionary achievement "based largely on innate dispositions (imagination, make-belief, play, narrative structuring and so forth). Storytelling is mastered at an early age in a child's individual development. Learning the practice is learning to utilize these dispositions for specific communicative ends" (Lamarque and Stein, *Truth* 33).
[114] Bruner, *Making Stories* 86f.
[115] Bruner, *Making Stories* 103.
[116] MacIntyre, *After Virtue* 203ff.

and family, [...] institutions, [...] the past, [...] reference groups."[117] Our *self-narratives* are never told in monologue from one perspective only, but are made up of a Bakhtinian polyphony of voices speaking from different perspectives.

Fictional storytelling is especially suited to portray the chorus of voices involved in the narrative creation of the modern *self*. "Literariness", or "novelness" (*romannost*) in Bakhtin's terms, is characterised by "a dialogical exchange taking place on several different levels at the same time",[118] including "the dialogue between an author, his characters, and his audience, as well as [...] the dialogue of readers with the characters and their author."[119] The "act of reading",[120] to borrow Wolfgang Iser's terminology, always includes a multitude of horizons or languages of heteroglossia, each of them, as Bakhtin puts it, "carry[ing] with them their own expression, their own evaluative tone, which we assimilate, re-work, and re-accentuate."[121] By comparing our past with our present experience as we read, we enter into what Wayne C. Booth calls a process of "coduction", i.e. a conversation with the many voices of the other potentially included in the text, modifying our previous knowledge in the encounter.[122]

In his defence of ethical criticism, Booth argues that literature introduces the reader to a multitude of conceptual horizons seldom encountered in similar density in "real" life. Each fictional narrative "provides an alternative story set in a created 'world' that is itself a fresh alternative to the 'world' or 'worlds' previously serving as boundaries of the reader's imagination."[123] In contrast to what we call reality, however, our encounter with the other of literary texts, does not entail any direct practical choice for the *self* in the "real" world of social interaction. Instead, literature furnishes us with a fertile testing ground for (moral) ideas. It supplies us with a great number of possible versions of the good life offered to us in the form of "relatively cost-free [...] trial runs."[124] Each

---

[117] Bruner, *Making Stories* 78. Cf. MacIntyre, *After Virtue* 197ff.

[118] Michael Holquist, *Dialogism: Bakhtin and his World* (London: Routledge, 1990) 68.

[119] Holquist, *Dialogism* 69. Note in this context that we neither reject the concept of the author as Barthes and Foucault do, nor adhere to the "traditional" model of privileged, omniscient authorial authorship. Rather, we hold that the implied author of a literary text is "a decentred yet individual subject that can only be defined as the focal point of the multiple elements that make up its horizon" (Antor, "Ethical Plurivocity" 29). Cf. Wayne C. Booth, *The Rhetoric of Fiction* (1961; Chicago: The University of Chicago Press, 1965) 71ff and 211ff.

[120] Wolfgang Iser, *Der Akt des Lesens* (München: UTB, 1976).

[121] Quoted in Brandon R. Kershner, "Mikhail Bakhtin and Bakhtinian Criticism," *Introducing Literary Theories: A Guide and Glossary*, ed. Julian Wolfreys (Edinburgh: Edinburgh UP, 2001) 22.

[122] Booth, *Company* 71ff.

[123] Booth, *Company* 17.

[124] Booth, *Company* 485.

work of literature invites us to take part in a "conversational gambit."[125] It tempts us to let our *selves* be "occupied by a foreign imaginary world",[126] induces us to compare our habitual horizons and frameworks of belief with the new horizons on offer and to play them off against one another. In other words, literary narrative entices us to distance ourselves from ossified beliefs and rigid patterns of thought, it tempts us to search for fresh capacities, for possible new ways of conferring meaning and substance on the story of our lives.

Still, as Booth reminds us, we do well to carefully appraise the literary company we keep, refraining from making all offered horizons our own and letting our *selves* completely and uncritically dissolve in alterity.[127] Bruner conspicuously points out that "[t]he art of the possible is a perilous art. It must take heed of life as we know it, yet alienate us sufficiently to tempt us into thinking of alternatives beyond it. It challenges as it comforts."[128] If the individual *self* is ever to be 'at one' with its respective life choices, 'at-one-ment' will be achieved via a pragmatic, critical "pluralism with limits",[129] characterised by the taking on as well as the discarding of offered ideas. It is to this peculiarly postmodern challenge which we will turn in our discussion of Ian McEwan's novels.

---

[125] Antor, "Ethical Plurivocity" 42. Cf. Booth, *Company* 207.
[126] Booth, *Company* 139.
[127] Booth, *Company* 265.
[128] Bruner, *Making Stories* 94.
[129] Booth, *Company* 489.

2. Setting the Scene: The Postmodern Challenge to the *Self*

2.1 A Whole Supermarket of Theories: Exploring the Panorama of Ian McEwan's Novels

The late 1970s and early 1980s marked "an important point of departure in [...] British fiction, the clear emergence of a new generation or grouping of writers and of new concerns in fiction."[130] Dissatisfied with postmodernism as "a culture of pastiche, depthless intertextuality and hermeneutic break with the real",[131] the "Brit Pack"[132] of the 1980s and 1990s - including writers like Martin Amis, Graham Swift, Julian Barnes, Kazuo Ishiguro, and Ian McEwan - turned to innovative forms of plot-orientated storytelling that combined a pronounced interest in contemporary (British) culture and (recent) history with a concern for social and ethical questions. Like the narrator in Graham Swift's *Waterland* (1983), the rising generation of British novelists of the 1980s was keenly aware of the fact that man is "the animal that craves meaning" (*W* 140) and that storytelling, by throwing a net over the random nature of experience, caters to this yearning.

However, our ineradicable need for patterns of meaning and orientation is countered in our post-metaphysical age by the unsettling awareness of the relative validity of value commitments, the constructedness of all frameworks of belief, and the heterogeneity of local narratives. Novels like Ian McEwan's *The Child in Time*, *Black Dogs*, *Enduring Love*, and *Atonement* draw the reader's attention to the difficulty, complexity, and relativity of value commitments in a world where prescriptive master narratives have been debunked. On the formal level, "the paradox of the desire for and the suspicion of narrative mastery – and master narratives"[133] manifests itself in the merging of a basic narrative realism with metafictional elements. Hence, novels by authors like Martin Amis, Graham Swift, Julian Barnes, Kazuo Ishiguro, and Ian McEwan evoke the existence of a real and familiar world outside the text in which the respective story could have taken place, but involve at the same time a significant degree of metafictional self-consciousness about their status as fiction.

---

[130] David Malcolm, *Understanding Ian McEwan* (Columbia: University of South Carolina Press, 2002) 6. Cf. Ansgar Nünning, *Der englische Roman des 20. Jahrhunderts*, Uni-Wissen Anglistik, Amerikanistik (Stuttgart: Klett, 1998) 91.
[131] Marc Delrez, "Escape into Innocence: Ian McEwan and the Nightmare of History," *Ariel - A Review of International English Literature* 26.2 (1995): 7.
[132] Slay, *Ian McEwan* 4.
[133] Hutcheon, *Politics* 64.

Ian McEwan has established himself in the *pantheon* of contemporary British novelists as an imaginative representative of the literary trends that characterised the British novel in the last decades of the twentieth century. Like the authors mentioned above, Ian McEwan concedes that "there's a certain kind of [...] visual reality"[134] that can be put into words and conveyed to the reader. He believes "that events in the past did actually happen, and that there are truths that approximate to descriptions of [reality] that are better than others."[135] At the same time, however, he denies the existence of an objective master version of reality that can claim universal validity. In *The Child in Time*, for instance, theoretical physicist Thelma challenges traditional Newtonian assumptions about objective, stable reality in her meditations on wave and particle functions, quantum leaps, and space time. Thelma treats the main character Stephen to "a whole supermarket of theories" (*CT* 115),[136] explaining that

> [o]ne offering has the world dividing every infinitesimal fraction of a second into *an infinite number of possible versions* [emphasis mine], constantly branching and proliferating, with consciousness neatly picking its way through to create the illusion of stable reality. (*CT* 115)

Still, at the formal level of novelistic construction, *The Child in Time*, *Black Dogs*, *Enduring Love*, and *Atonement* are characterised by a "dense, close-grained surface realism"[137] which takes as its touchstone an empiricist understanding of the world according to which physical reality is accessible in an objective fashion. In an interview conducted in 1989, McEwan pointed out that his preference for realist transparencies over "duplicitous evasions"[138] has a practical function at the level of day-to-day living, that "[w]e continue, of course, to live within a Newtonian universe – [that] its physics are perfectly adequate to describe and measure the world we can see; only the very large and the very small are beyond its grasp."[139] It appears that just as neurobiological evidence cannot dismantle our concept of stable and coherent selfhood, the theories advanced by theoretical physics do not invalidate our everyday notion of an objectively perceptible physical world surrounding us.

Disorientation and doubt in Ian McEwan's novels largely remain at the level of the characters' inner - i.e. psychological, emotional, and mental - world and are set off against a clearly mapped out temporal and geographical

---

[134] Adam Hunt, "Ian McEwan," *B&A: New Fiction* 21 (1996): 49.
[135] Hunt, "Ian McEwan" 49.
[136] Henceforth abbreviated in quotations as *CT* (*Child in Time*), *BD* (*Black Dogs*), *EL* (*Enduring Love*), and *A* (*Atonement*).
[137] Derek Wright, "New Physics, Old Metaphysics: Quantum and Quotidian in Ian McEwan's *The Child in Time*," *Revista alicantina de estudios ingleses* 10 (1997): 231.
[138] Wright, "Physics" 231.
[139] McEwan quoted in: Wright, "Physics" 231.

background. *The Child in Time*, for instance, though set a few years in the future from its time of publication in 1987, presents us with a recognisable version of 1980s Thatcherite Britain.[140] The right-wing tendencies of 1980s laissez-faire capitalism have been taken further with licensed begging (*CT* 2), an armed police force (*CT* 35), and schools sold off to private investors (*CT* 23). Still, the dystopic elements running through the novel do not violate the basic conventions of realism, since they appear to be "logical developments of British government policy in the 1980s, especially that associated with the governments of Margaret Thatcher",[141] i.e. they constitute disturbing, but possible deviations from British empirical reality at the time of the novel's publication. Written in the tradition of the memoir-novel,[142] *Black Dogs* is impressed with the hallmark of verisimilitude, supplying us with exact historical dates and depicting locations that can be pointed out on a good map of the respective area. So, for instance, we witness the dismantling of the Berlin Wall on 9 November 1989, following the first person narrator Jeremy and his father-in-law Bernard on their tour from Kreuzberg to the Victory Monument, the Brandenburg Gate (*BD* 82), and Checkpoint Charlie (*BD* 88). An almost "hermetically English"[143] novel, *Enduring Love* is set in London and Oxfordshire in the 1990s, taking us, for instance, to Heathrow Airport (*EL* 4), the Chiltern Hills (*EL* 5), the Reading Room of the London Library (*EL* 40), Maida Vale (*EL* 54), Bloomsbury (*EL* 69), and Watlington (*EL* 220). The stress on historical and political realism observed in *The Child in Time* and *Black Dogs* is shifted in *Enduring Love* to a psychological realism, focussing on the nuanced, accurate portrayal of pathological love and taking us inside the minds of psychologically disturbed Jed Parry, his victim Joe Rose, and Joe's partner Clarissa. The psychological authenticity of Jed Parry's pathological love for Joe is corroborated by the

---

[140] The critical discussion of Thatcherism found its way into a considerable number of British novels written in the 1980s. So, for example, David Loge's *Nice Work* (1988), Pat Barker's *Union Street* (1982) and *The Century's Daughter* (1986), or Martin Amis's *Money: A Suicide Note* (1984) and *London Fields* (1989) critically engage with the social conditions of Britain in the 1980s. Cf. Ansgar Nünning. "Zwischen der realistischen Erzähltradition und der experimentellen Poetik des Postmodernismus: Erscheinungsformen und Entwicklungstendenzen des englischen Romans seit dem zweiten Weltkrieg aus gattungstheoretischer Perspektive," *Eine andere Geschichte der englischen Literatur: Epochen, Gattungen und Teilgebiete im Überblick*, ed. Monika Fludernik und Ansgar Nünning, WVT-Handbücher zum literaturwissenschaftlichen Studium 2 (Trier: WVT, 1996) 219.
[141] Malcolm, *Understanding* 96.
[142] i.e. a novel that purports to be a "true" (auto)biography or memoir but which is wholly or mostly fictitious. As a literary form or convention, the memoir emerged in the eighteenth century with novels such as Daniel Defoe's *Moll Flanders* (1722) and John Cleland's *Fanny Hill: Memoirs of a Lady of Pleasure* (1748-49). Cuddon, *Dictionary* 539.
[143] Malcolm, *Understanding* 9.

rendering of three of his love letters to Joe and above all by the printing of a spoof article on de Clérambault's syndrome from the *British Review of Psychiatry* in appendix I of the novel (*EL* 233-243). In Part Two of *Atonement*, Robbie Turner's march to Dunkirk in 1940 is replenished with geographical detail and warfare minutiae. With the aid of Robbie's rear area map (*A* 191) we follow the English army's slow retreat to the Bergues-Furnes canal (*A* 225); we learn details about Stuka attacks (*A* 236-238), the German Luftwaffe (*A* 214), "marshalling centres, warrant officers behind makeshift desks, rubber stamps and dockets" (*A* 274).

Although firmly part of the special dynamism that characterised the English novel in the 1980s and 1990s, Ian McEwan proves to be an exceedingly versatile writer who persistently resists being pinned down and classified. In an interview conducted shortly after the publication of his second collection of short stories, *In Between the Sheets*, and his first novel, *The Cement Garden*, McEwan claimed: "I certainly can't locate myself inside any shared, any sort of community taste, aesthetic ambition or critical position or anything else. I don't really feel part of anything at all."[144] McEwan has come a long way since the beginning of his writing career and the detailed, graphic depictions of "dirt, scum, pus, menstrual blood, pathetic obesity, total chinlessness, enforced transvestism, early teenage incest, child abuse and [...] murder"[145] in his two collections of short stories and his early novels. With *The Child in Time*, McEwan moved on from a claustrophobic world of sexual and social aberrations to a fiction openly engaging in complex ethical, social, and historical issues.[146] The ethical turn in McEwan's writing career - brought about by the awareness that "nobody hangs free"[147] of value commitments - echoes the insights formulated by ethical critics in the late 1980s and early 1990s. It is thus part of a greater cultural movement which endeavours to open-mindedly address inescapable questions of value and which regards imaginative literature as an indispensable partner in this enterprise. Goaded on by ontological and epistemological questions like "Who am I?" and "Where am I going?", the protagonists of McEwan's mature fiction struggle to position themselves in a

---

[144] Christopher Ricks, "Adolescence and After - An Interview with Ian McEwan," *Listener* 110 (1979): 527.

[145] Robert Towers (1979) quoted in Slay, *Ian McEwan* 9.

[146] For a discussion of the turn in McEwan's writing career refer to: Malcolm, *Understanding* 4f; Slay, *Ian McEwan* 34; Ryan Kiernan, *Ian McEwan, Writers and Their Work*, ed. Isabel Armstrong (Plymouth UK: Northcote House/ The British Council, 1994) 2; Jürgen Schlaeger, "Who's Afraid of Ian McEwan?" *Beyond Borders: Re-defining Generic and Ontological Boundaries*, ed. Ramón Plo-Alastrué and María Jesús Martínez-Alfaro (Heidelberg: C.Winter, 2002) 189f.

[147] McEwan quoted in: Adam Begley, "The Art of Fiction CLXXIII," *The Paris Review* 162 (2002), 10 Apr. 2003 <http:// www.parisreview.com/ tpr162/mcewan1.html>.

world where "the Charybdis of new-fangled arbitrary valuelessness"[148] constantly rears its ugly head.

However, Ian McEwan did not miraculously transform from a writer "obsessed with the perverse, the grotesque, the macabre"[149] into a social or moral prophet in the mid-1980s. Dark nightmares still haunt his mature fiction and his characters' postmodern condition is marked by a pervasive sense of alienation and disorientation. Contingency enters the protagonists' lives in the form of single, disturbing events that turn out to have unpredictable, far-reaching consequences in their lives, threatening the integrity of selfhood, frustrating their "desire to belong" (*CT* 60), shaking their confidence in accustomed beliefs, and endangering the stability of intimate relationships.

In *The Child in Time*, the abduction of Stephen Lewis's three-year-old daughter Kate on a routine trip to the supermarket all but leads to the destruction of his marriage to Julie and opens up a menacing epistemological void in his life that alienates him from any sense of consistent selfhood and belonging: "Nothing was his own, not his strokes or his movement, not the calling sounds, not even the sadness, nothing was nothing's own" (*CT* 57). A chance encounter with two terrifying *Black Dogs* during her honeymoon trip to southern France in 1946 changes June Tremaine's life for ever. The confrontation with the fierce animals triggers an unresolved debate between rationalism and mysticism that undermines June's marriage to Bernard and reverberates in the life of her son-in-law Jeremy, who tries to fill "the emotional void, the feeling of belonging nowhere and to no one" (*BD* 18) by writing down the story of June's life. *Enduring Love* opens with a random meeting between popular-science writer Joe Rose and religiously obsessed Jed Parry during a fatal ballooning accident in the Vale of Oxford. Joe, Jed, and three other men try to rescue a young boy trapped in the basket of a helium balloon that is being dragged along the ground by the wind. The men, holding on to the ropes attached to the balloon, are suddenly lifted off the ground by a strong gust of wind. When one of them lets go, the others jump off one by one. Only John Logan, father of two, hangs on to his rope, the balloon surges upwards, and Logan finally falls. The harrowing encounter with senseless death turns into a nightmare of persecution and harassment which shakes Joe's belief in the master narrative of science and results in the slow disintegration of his formerly happy relationship with his partner Clarissa. In *Atonement*, thirteen-year-old Briony Tallis ruins the lives of two people by misinterpreting the events of one hot summer's day in 1935. She spends the rest of her life trying to atone for her youthful mistake, finally coming to realise "a simple, obvious thing she had always known, and everyone

---

[148] Antor, "Ethics" 66.
[149] Malcolm, *Understanding* 4.

knew: that a person is, among all else, a material thing, easily torn, not easily mended" (*A* 304).

However fragile and endangered consistent selfhood has become in a universe of contingent forces, McEwan's characters do not abandon the quest for the good life, but remain inside an ongoing discourse of values. *The Child in Time*, *Black Dogs*, and *Enduring Love* are novels of ideas in which different versions of the world are juxtaposed, or in Charles Taylor's terms, where different "qualitative frameworks"[150] collide and battles are fought out over incommensurable explanatory patterns. In *The Child in Time*, for example, Stephen's artistic imagination is confronted with "a whole supermarket of theories" (*CT* 115) about chaos and relativity, in *Black Dogs*, mysticism and scepticism are set off against each other, and *Enduring Love* takes up the two cultures debate between science and literature, opposing at the same time the epistemologies of science and religion.

McEwan's latest novel *Atonement* constitutes a departure from the novel of ideas into the terrain of character and emotions. As McEwan stated in an interview conducted in 2002:

> I think I've come to an end of a cycle of novels with *Enduring Love*, which began with *The Child in Time*, included *Black Dogs* and *The Innocent*. Those were novels in which ideas were played out. They are, among other things, novels of ideas. Both *Amsterdam* and *Atonement* are moving off in another direction. I suppose that emotions […] will mean more to me. […] I think that I might push forward in my own little projects to make my novels more character led […]. When I got to the end of *Atonement* I felt that Briony was the most complete person I'd ever conjured, and I'd like to do that again and take it further.[151]

McEwan's move from a reflective, philosophical engagement with conflicting "ideas" in his novels of the 1980s and mid-1990s to a focus on character and emotions in his latest works, coincides with a subtle shift of emphasis that can be currently observed in ethical criticism. While literary critics of the late 1980s and early 1990s decried the exile of evaluation in their domain and tried to achieve an open acknowledgement of the necessity of value commitments, "the terms 'value', 'ethics', and 'aesthetics' have [today] become the privileged centrepieces of all theoretical vocabularies."[152] With evaluative reading well established within the literary academy, ethical criticism now sets out to broaden its thematic horizon by incorporating new aspects into existing theories. In *Upheavals of Thought* (2001), for example, Martha Nussbaum takes the ethics

---

[150] Taylor, *Sources* 25.
[151] Margaret Reynolds and Jonathan Noakes, *Ian McEwan: The Essential Guide* (London: Vintage, 2002) 23.
[152] Steven Connor, "After Cultural Value: Ecology, Ethics, Aesthetics," *Ethics and Aesthetics: The Moral Turn of Postmodernism*, ed. Gerhard Hoffmann, and Alfred Hornung (Heidelberg: C. Winter, 1996) 1.

debate into a new direction by positing that there can be no adequate ethical criticism without an adequate theory of the emotions. According to Nussbaum, emotions such as fear, love, grief, guilt, or loss are no mindless animal energies, but "forms of evaluative judgement that ascribe to certain things and persons outside a person's own control great importance for the person's own flourishing."[153] As "value-laden ways of understanding the world",[154] emotions are ineradicably part of our accounts of a complete human life, they essentially contribute to the *ethos* or character of the individual *self*. By focussing on Briony's intense feelings of guilt as she tells and re-tells the story of her life, *Atonement* reveals Briony's value-laden way of understanding the world, rendering her perspective of events with "a degree of self-consciousness which far exceeds that found in any of [McEwan's] previous novels."[155]

2.2 Rising to the Challenge: Narrative (*Self-*)Creation

So far, we have sketched out some striking landmarks in the complex panorama of Ian McEwan's novels. It has been argued that *The Child in Time*, *Black Dogs*, *Enduring Love*, and *Atonement* are characterised by a keen awareness of the epistemological problem of providing definite answers to the inescapable question "How should one live?" At the same time, we noted a reluctance on the part of the author to embody these problems at the formal level of storytelling. Indeed, we pointed out McEwan's willingness to provide the reader with unproblematic, realist narratives whose clearly mapped out geographical and temporal landscape constitutes the contrastive foil against which the characters' disorientation and alienation is projected. As in everyday life, narrative in Ian McEwan's novels functions as a tool for dealing with the challenge presented to us by contingency. It constitutes a means of turning "the generally unstoried world that meets us daily [...] into [a] meaning-ridden story."[156] As McEwan observes: "The random element in life is a gift to the novelist to make a pattern of it, to make some sense of it, to contest its meaning or even ask whether there's any meaning to it at all."[157]

In other words, patterns of meaning are not inherent in the world but narratively created and recreated. As Rorty laconically observes: "The world

---

[153] Martha C. Nussbaum, *Upheavals of Thought: The Intelligence of Emotions* (Cambridge: Cambridge UP, 2001) 22.
[154] Nussbaum, *Upheavals* 88.
[155] Brian Finney, "Briony's Stand".
[156] Booth, *Company* 192.
[157] Eric Schoeck, "An Interview with Ian McEwan," *Capitola Book Café*, 16 Feb. 1998, 10 Dec. 2002 <http://www.capitolabookcafe.com/andrea/mcewan.html>.

does not speak. Only we do."[158] In the novels discussed in this paper, Ian McEwan reminds us of this fact by alluding to the fictionality, i.e. the constructed nature, of his writing and by making his protagonists writers and tellers, i.e. creators, of stories.[159] Events in the novels do not seem to narrate themselves, but are embodied in a discourse that takes into account the many-voicedness of a world where meaning is not simply found or painstakingly unearthed, but constantly constructed and reconstructed from random data and from changing points of view. In an interview conducted shortly after the publication of *Atonement*, McEwan states:

> I think that I am always drawn to some kind of balance between a fiction that is self-reflective on its own processes, and one that has a forward impetus too, that will completely accept the given terms of the illusion of fiction. I've never been interested in that kind of fiction that triumphantly declares that art is not life. [...] Readers never have any problem with it. But I do have an interest in something self-reflective along the way.[160]

Thus, although McEwan's novels remain true to the realist convention of evoking a lifelike illusion of a real world outside the text, they repeatedly reflect on the process involved in the narrative creation of this world.

In *The Child in Time*, Stephen becomes aware of the pattern-building, meaning-giving power inherent in narrative when he returns to London "after a hashish-befuddled tour of Turkey, Afghanistan and the North-West Frontier Province" (*CT* 23) in the early 1970s. He states that

> the work ethics he and his generation had worked so hard to destroy was still strong within him. *He craved order and purpose.* He took a cheap bedsit, found a job as a filing clerk in a news cutting agency and *set about writing a novel* [emphases mine]. (*CT* 23)

---

[158] Rorty, *Contingency* 6.

[159] Note in this context that the division made between art and life led to a critical debate about the terminology used when referring to the personages of fictional texts. Henry James observed that "characters [in a novel] are based on life but not to be confused with it" (Aleid Fokkema, *Postmodern Characters. A Study of Characterization in British and American Postmodern Fiction.* Amsterdam: Rodopi, 1991. 20). In keeping with James's interpretation, the characters of McEwan's novels are not 'people' or *selves* in the sense that living human beings are *selves* or people, but virtual human beings intimately related, yet not to be confused with empirical human beings. Similarly, Booth points out that we must remain aware of the distinction between fictional and non-fictional narrative, between empirical persons and fictional characters, because "we read differently when we believe that a story claims to be true than when we take it as 'made up' " (Booth, *Company* 16).

[160] Reynolds and Noakes, *Ian McEwan* 20.

Two years after his daughter's abduction, Stephen, now firmly established in literary circles as a successful writer of children's books (*CT* 22), is involved in the "Sub-committee on Reading and Writing" (*CT* 4) of the British government's "Official Commission for Childcare" (*CT* 3). The latter consists of a group of specialists meeting on a regular basis to compile an *Authorised Childcare Handbook* (*CT* 1) commissioned by the Prime Minister. During a debate about early literacy, the question arises whether the high degree of abstraction involved in reading and writing - i.e. the reduction of "limitless intellectual, emotional, intuitive resource[s]" (*CT* 72) to a limited number of graphic symbols - "shatters the unity of the child's world view [and] drives a fatal wedge between the word and the thing that the word names" (*CT* 73).

Justifying himself as a writer of children's books, Stephen argues that early literacy does not sever the relationship between "self and world" (*CT* 74) as his opponent claims, but on the contrary, by furnishing the child with a useful tool of abstraction, facilitates access to a world of otherwise uncharted diversity.[161] Thus, Stephen claims:

> *[T]he written word can be the very means by which the world and the self connect* [emphasis mine], which is why the very best writing for children has about it a quality of invisibility, of taking you right through to the things it names, and through metaphors and imagery can evoke feelings, smells, impressions for which there are no words at all [...]. The written word is no less part of what it names than the spoken word. (*CT* 75)[162]

In his speech to the commission, Stephen pleads for a basic realism in children's literature that helps children label, name, and pattern a world they recognise as familiar, but which at the same time exposes them to a "foreign imaginary world",[163] evoking feelings, smells and impressions for which there are no words at all.

Similarly, in *Black Dogs* and *Enduring Love*, narrative serves as a tool wielded by the protagonists to invest their lives with meaning, to connect *self*

---

[161] Stephen's definition of language as a system of abstract signs referring to the world outside this sign-system echoes the structuralist conception of language devised by the French linguist Ferdinand de Saussure in a set of lectures at the Sorbonne and posthumously published by his students as *Cours de linguistique générale* in 1916. Thus, Sassure holds: "Sprache [ist] ein präzis erfassbares, formal exakt darstellbares relationelles System von formalen [...] Elementen [...]" (Hadumod Bußmann, *Lexikon der Sprachwissenschaft*, Kröners Taschenausgabe Bd. 452. Stuttgart: Kröner, 1990. 743).

[162] Stephen's plea for literary realism mirrors Briony Tallis's early notion of prose fiction: "A story was direct and simple, allowing nothing to come between herself and the reader [...]. Reading a sentence and understanding it were the same thing. [...] You saw the word *castle* and it was there, seen from some distance, with the woods in high summer spread before it [...]" (*A* 37).

[163] Booth, *Company* 139.

and world, in fact, to (re)create them*selves* by constructing their personal story from the abundant material on offer. In the course of this enterprise, narrative is thematised time and again, drawing the reader's attention to the constructedness of all explanatory systems. At the beginning of *Black Dogs*, Jeremy, orphaned at the age of eight, is drifting along as an "abandoned child" (*BD* 9), an orphan with no story to call his own. As Richard Pedot remarks:

> [L]e narrateur de la biographie des Tremaine se pose d'entrée de jeu comme un orphelin postmoderne, orphelin de tous les systèmes idéologiques qui ont montré leur faillite à rendre compte des abîmes de l'âme humaine.[164]

Jeremy seeks to escape his postmodern rootlessness by connecting up to the various explanatory patterns or narratives on offer in the parental homes of his middle-class friends from school. Thus, he makes the acquaintance of "neo-Freudian psychoanalysts" (*BD* 12), is introduced to the narrative of science "in the big untidy house" of an oceanographer (*BD* 12), and discusses Proust, Heine, Thucydides, and Scott-Moncrieff in the "civilised, intellectually curious, open-minded" (*BD* 11) atmosphere of a diplomat's household.

Marrying into the Tremaine family, Jeremy, still longing for substitute parents to fill "the emotional void, the feeling of belonging nowhere and to no one" (*BD* 18), finally acquires "parents in the form of in-laws, June and Bernard Tremaine" (*BD* 18). Jeremy tries to understand his in-laws' diverging philosophical positions, but finds he cannot subscribe to either of their world-views (*BD* 19). Writing a memoir of June's life he enters into an "interior dialogue" with opposing narratives and tries to stake out the territory of his own belief. As David Malcolm points out, *Black Dogs* is characterised by a discursive, essay-like element that foregrounds the constructedness of all philosophical positions:

> The two positions – that of June (belief in some kind of deity, in some kind of intermittently benign order in the universe, in the spirit) and that of Bernard (an insistence on the importance of rationalism, on the absence of a controlling deity, on a material understanding of the world) – are set out in the novel, as if they were two possible views of the universe discussed in an essay.[165]

In the passage following Jeremy's encounter with a scorpion in June's house in southern France (*BD* 116), for example, the text develops a dialogical quality with June's and Bernard's imagined voices arguing about the existence or non-existence of a meaningful universe (*BD* 117-120): "Statements and counter-

---

[164] Richard Pedot, "Une narration en quête de son sujet: Chemin de l'écriture et écriture du chemin dans *Black Dogs* de Ian McEwan," *Études Britanniques Contemporaines* 11 (1997): 71.
[165] Malcolm, *Understanding* 137f.

statements chased their tails [...]. It was a drone that would not be banished. It continued even when I managed to turn my attention away" (*BD* 119). Throughout the novel, we are reminded of the fact that there is no philosophical ceiling-view to be gained from which one can safely judge all (moral) positions, but that our divergent perspectives on the world remain open to interpretation and re-interpretation in an ongoing discourse of values.

The clash of world-views or conflicting (master) narratives observed in *Black Dogs* is again of central interest in *Enduring Love*. Joe Rose, a populariser of scientific theories, is a tireless advocate of rationalism and materialism, believing in the "powers of rationality and deduction" (*EL* 216). Joe's partner Clarissa, an expert scholar on Keat's love poetry (*EL* 7), is driven by emotions rather than by logic and reason, and Jed Parry is a mystic, "a man whose religious convictions are central to his delusions" (*EL* 233). First person narrator Joe[166] self-consciously makes use of narrative to structure his experiences and to construct meaningful patterns from random (physical) data. The opening sentence of the novel is one of a number that characterise a self-aware narrative, conscious of the way we transform an unstoried world into meaningful narrative patterns.[167] Thus, Joe tells us: "The beginning is simple to mark. We were in the sunlight under a turkey oak, partly protected from a strong, gusty wind. [...] This was the moment, this was the pinprick on the time map" (*EL* 1). A few pages later, Joe demonstrates his awareness of the structuring power inherent in storytelling when he states: "Let my freeze the frame [...] to describe our circle" (*EL* 12).

After their shattering encounter with death in the ballooning accident, Joe and Clarissa sit down at their kitchen table and try to tame the chaos of their emotions by moulding their experience into clearly demarcated narrative structures. As Joe puts it:

> I told [Clarissa] how [John Logan] seemed to hang in the air before dropping, and she told me how a scrap of Milton had flashed before her: *Hurled headlong flaming from th'Ethereal Sky*. But we backed away from that moment again and again, circling it, stalking it, until we had it cornered and began to tame it with words. (*EL* 29)

Joe turns to the language of science to describe the accident, slowing down John Logan's fall ("The best description of a reality does not need to mimic its

---

[166] *Enduring Love* is largely told from Joe's first person perspective, although on five occasions other narrators have their say. Chapter 23 takes the form of a letter from Clarissa to Joe. Clarissa's point of view is furthermore rendered in chapter 9; there however, she does not speak for herself, but Joe adopts her point of view to narrate the circumstances that led up to a bitter quarrel between him and Clarissa. Jed Parry's thoughts are presented to us directly on three occasions, each time through a letter he sent to Joe (chapters 11, 16, and appendix 2).

[167] Cf. Oliver Reynolds, "A Master of Accidents," *Times Literary Supplement*, 12 Sept. 1997: 12.

velocity", *EL* 17) and Clarissa chooses the vocabulary of literature ("She said it all again and repeated the lines from *Paradise Lost*", *EL* 30-31) to accommodate the harrowing experience. However, despite their differences of approach, both partners are equally aware of the vital structuring task narrative performs in their lives: "[W]e were back in our seats, leaning over the table like dedicated craftsmen at work, grinding the jagged edge of memories, hammering the unspeakable into forms of words, threading single perceptions into narrative [...]" (*EL* 30).

Atonement is in many ways a head-on engagement with storytelling. Thus, the novel discusses the nature of narrative construction and thematises literature as a subject matter. Strikingly, the novel opens with an ironic description, not of the protagonist Briony, but of the play she wrote at the age of thirteen to celebrate her brother Leon's coming down from Cambridge. In other words, we are acquainted with an instance of Briony's literary imagination before we are introduced to her as a character:

> The play [...] was written by her in a two-day tempest of composition [...] At some moments chilling, at others desperately sad, the play told a tale of the heart whose message, conveyed in a rhyming prologue, was that love which did not build a foundation on good sense was doomed. (*A* 3)

On the surface, *Atonement* appears to be a "classic" example of realist storytelling. The long first part of the novel, for instance, depicts the events of one hot English summer's day leading up to the rape of Briony's fifteen-year-old cousin Lola in the grounds of the Tallises' estate and culminates in Briony's false accusation of Robbie Turner, next door neighbour and friend of the family, who is arrested by the police on the morning of the following day.[168] Reading closer, however, we find that we are presented with a narrative that self-consciously (re)constructs a series of turning points in the career of Briony the writer, mirroring the stages Western literature went through in the course of the centuries:

> Six decades later [Briony] would describe how at the age of thirteen she had written her way through a whole history of literature, beginning with stories derived from the European tradition of folk tales, through drama with simple moral intent, to arrive at an impartial psychological realism which she had discovered, one special morning during a heat wave in 1935. (*A* 41)

---

[168] As we learn in Part Three of *Atonement*, Paul Marshall, another friend of the Tallis family turns out to be Lola's rapist. However, owing to Briony's accusation of Robbie, he gets away with his crime and marries Lola after the Second World War, while Robbie spends three years in Wandsworth prison 'atoning' for a crime he did not commit.

On that "special morning" Briony witnesses a mysterious encounter between her sister Cecilia and Cecilia's childhood friend Robbie by the fountain in the park of the family's estate. Briony looks on uncomprehendingly from the nursery window as her elder sister strips down to her underwear, dives into the pond, resurfaces, climbs out again, picks up a vase of flowers placed on the ground near the fountain, and sets off towards the house (*A* 39). Watching the scene by the fountain, Briony experiences a Joycean epiphany, a "kind of revelation" (*A* 41), about many-voicedness in a world where "truth has become as ghostly as an invention" (*A* 41). She is intrigued by the possibility of writing down the scene she has witnessed but cannot place "from three points of view" (*A* 39) as an impartial observer; freed from "the cumbrous struggle between good and bad, heroes and villains [...]" (*A* 39), relieved that "[s]he need not judge" (*A* 39) what is beyond her understanding.

However, Briony has to painfully learn that nothing and no-one can deliver her from the "cumbrous struggle" of placing herself in moral space and that, even if the Truth cannot be told, there still exists a possibility of misinterpreting events. Looking back on her early experiments with modernist writing, Briony asks herself: "Did she really think she could hide behind some borrowed notions of modern writing, and drown her guilt in a stream – three streams! – of consciousness?" (*A* 320). Indeed, the novel's coda reveals that we have not read an impartial account of reality written by a "hidden observer" (*A* 39), but the last version of "half a dozen different drafts" (*A* 369) composed by a guilt-ridden 77-year-old Briony in 1999. In this final draft the ageing author makes a last attempt at atoning for her fatal misinterpretation of reality in 1935 by narratively creating a reunion between Cecilia and Robbie in 1940 which in "reality" never took place as both lovers were already dead by that time.[169] Thus, in the very last chapter of the novel the realist illusions created on the preceding 350 or so pages are shattered and we are reminded of the fact that we have read a fictional account of (re)constructed events told by a narrator who is also the story's author, who has in turn been created by a novelist called Ian McEwan.

---

[169] Note that there is not even any definite clarity about the "fact" that Robbie and Cecilia actually died in the war. As Briony tells us in 1999: "I can no longer think what purpose would be served if, *say* [emphasis mine], I tried to persuade the reader, by direct or indirect means, that Robbie Turner died of septicaemia at Bray Dunes on 1 June 1940, or that Cecilia was killed in September of the same year by the bomb that destroyed Balham underground station" (*A* 370).

3. Unfolding the Map of Life: Locating the *Self*

3.1 Being a *Self* to Yourself: Identity and Orientation

In the previous chapter we traced the connection between narrative creation and the creation of meaning in Ian McEwan's *The Child in Time, Black Dogs, Enduring Love*, and *Atonement*. We observed that storytelling functions as an indispensable means of connecting *self* and world and stated that the protagonists in McEwan's novels create and recreate them*selves* by turning the complex, unstoried world they encounter into meaningful narratives. In the following, we will extend this picture by focussing on the concept of the *self* implicit in the discussion of narrative creation. What does "being a *self* to yourself" imply in Ian McEwan's fictional universe?

To begin with, McEwan's protagonists possess a sense of inwardness or inner depth and the related notion that they are *selves*.[170] Furthermore, they aspire to a unity and wholeness in their lives which can be specified in MacIntyre's terminology as "the unity of a narrative quest."[171] To be on a quest, however, presupposes some kind of *telos* or aim towards which the individual search is directed, i.e. it implies a positioning of the *self* in moral space and a sense of orientation towards "a believable framework as the object of the quest."[172] Taylor points out that "our orientation in relation to the good not only requires some framework(s) which define(s) the shape of the qualitatively higher, but also a sense of where we stand in relation to this."[173] Accordingly, McEwan's characters are either in search of new patterns of orientation, trying to place them*selves* in relation to some good, or they possess frameworks of belief which, as structuring grids in their lives, guide their choices and decisions in individual instances.

As we have seen in the previous chapter, the protagonists of McEwan's novels universally turn to narrative to transform the random data supplied by experience into meaningful patterns. Their stories differ, however, because they are told from different perspectives or outlooks on the world. As Dan Slobin remarks:

> One cannot verbalize experience without taking a *perspective*, and [...] the language being used often favours particular perspectives. The world does not present 'events'

---

[170] Taylor, *Sources* x.
[171] MacIntyre, *After Virtue* 203.
[172] Taylor, *Sources* 17.
[173] Taylor, *Sources* 42.

to be encoded in language. Rather, in the process of speaking and writing, experiences are filtered through language into *verbalized events*.[174]

When Jeremy in *Black Dogs* remembers his "adolescent self" (*BD* 14), for example, he filters his past experiences through the particular literary language he used at that time, consciously mimicking "the rather formal, distancing, labyrinthine tone in which [he] used to speak, clumsily derived from [his] scant reading of Proust which was supposed to announce [him] to the world as an intellectual" (*BD* 14). Encoding events in language and taking a "unique [...] first person point of view",[175] however, depends on our ability to discriminate *self* from non-*self*, to distinguish between our recollections and those of other people. Eakin refers to the vital, *self*-referential function of memory when he states that "every recollection refers not only to the remembered event or person or object but to the person who is remembering."[176]

Although, as post-Enlightenment Western moderns, we are aware that neither the world nor the *self* have an intrinsic or divine nature, selfhood "cannot but come to feel fixed and unchallengeable, whatever our knowledge of history and cultural variation may lead us to believe."[177] Despite neurobiological evidence to the contrary we are loath to abandon the notion that selfhood comprises some essential essence or vital element, "anchored in the very nature of the human agent",[178] distinguishing us from animals and inanimate objects. Thus, when Joe stumbles across John Logan's body sitting upright and motionless in a field after the ballooning accident in *Enduring Love*, he states:

> I became aware that what I had taken for calmness was *absence*. There was no one there. The quietness was that of the inanimate, and I understood again, because I had seen dead bodies before, why a pre-scientific age would have needed to invent the soul. It was no less clear than the evening sun sinking through the sky. The closing down of countless interrelated neural and bio-chemical exchanges combined to suggest to the naked *eye the illusion of the extinguished spark, or the simple departure of a single necessary element* [emphasis mine]. However scientifically informed we count ourselves to be, fear and awe still surprise us in the presence of the dead. Perhaps it's life we're really wondering at. (*EL* 23)

In fact, we think that our thoughts, emotions, and ideas reside "inside" us, animate us from within, whereas "the objects in the world which these mental states bear on are 'without.' "[179] In *Atonement*, thirteen-year-old Briony

---

[174] Quoted in Bruner, *Making Stories* 73.
[175] Davidson, *Subjective* 89.
[176] Eakin, *How Our Lives Become Stories* 19.
[177] Taylor, *Sources* 112.
[178] Taylor, *Sources* 111.
[179] Taylor, *Sources* 111.

distinguishes between the outer form of the body and a "bright and private *inside* feeling" (*A* 36), an inner world of the *self* commanding her body and constituting the central, unchallengeable, "true" core of her identity. Contemplating her hand with detached interest, Briony wonders "how this thing, this machine for gripping, this fleshy spider on the end of her arm, came to be hers, entirely at her command" (*A* 35). Moving her forefinger, she marvels: "There was no stitching, no seam, and yet she knew that behind the smooth continuous fabric was the real self – was it her soul?" (*A* 36). Similarly, June Tremaine tells Jeremy in *Black Dogs* that what mattered in life was "to make the connection with this centre, this *inner being*, and then extend and deepen it. Then carry it *outwards* to others [emphases mine]" (*BD* 60).

Being "connected to, or in contact with, what [we] see as good, or of crucial importance, or of fundamental value"[180] is one of our basic human aspirations. We strive to be well-placed towards some good, talking of *self-fulfilment* or of "being whole" (*CT* 74) when we reach our objective, when we feel 'at one' with the life choices and decisions we have made. Throughout our lives we are on a quest for the good, conceiving of life as having a direction towards what we are not yet,[181] (re)making our*selves in via*. Identity formation, as Eakin observes, is "the lifelong process of making selves that we engage in daily."[182] Stephen Lewis in *The Child in Time* realises that in the contingent chaos of postmodern existence, even provisional, short-term destinations can be constitutive of "undamaged human personhood."[183] Thus, when Stephen rejoins the regular meetings of the Official Commission for Childcare after its autumn break, he states: "To have a destination, a place where you were expected, a shred of identity, was such a relief after a month of game shows and Scotch" (*CT* 132). By equating a destination or *telos* with identity, Stephen stresses the vital importance of structures of meaning and points of reference in our lives. Without a *telos*, we are lost without clear contours of identity in a space of empty contingency. Hence, in *Black Dogs*, Jeremy says about his rootless youth: "I had no attachments, I believed in nothing" (*BD* 19).

As pattern-building animals we feel whole only when we are firmly placed in relation to the goods we value. Knowing where we stand in moral space keeps our *selves* from falling apart, from losing the sense of rootedness, wholeness, and 'at-one-ment' we strive for in our lives. So, when Jeremy thinks of his wife and children during a trip to Southern France in 1989, he feels that he has finally found the "hearth" (e.g. *BD* 15, 17) he had been vainly searching for as a boy. He states: "A thousand miles away, in or near one house among all the millions, were Jenny and our four children, my tribe. I belonged, my life was

---

[180] Taylor, *Sources* 42.
[181] Taylor, *Sources* 48.
[182] Eakin, *How Our Lives Become Stories* 1.
[183] Taylor, *Sources* 27.

rooted and rich" (*BD* 122). In our aspirations to fullness, substance, and wholeness, certain hypergoods or values - such as family life in Jeremy's case - provide spiritual landmarks which help us assess our lives as we move forward into the future or look back to the past. Taylor reminds us that "we only know ourselves through the history of [our] maturations and regressions, overcomings and defeats. [Our] self-understanding necessarily has temporal depth and incorporates narrative [...]."[184]

In analogy to orientation in physical space, successful orientation in moral space depends on a map or framework of belief as well as on our knowledge of where we are placed on this map, i.e. of where we are positioned in relation to the hypergoods and values that guide our progress.[185] Having once attained orientation in moral space, our framework definitions provide "the horizon within which we know where we stand, and what meaning things have for us."[186] In *Black Dogs*, Jeremy draws on the spatial metaphor of orientation when he talks about "the metaphorical landscape" (*BD* 140) of Bernard and June's future. Sitting on the Dolmen de la Prunarède, the newly-weds begin "an exited discussion [...] in which their route the next day across this glorious alien countryside became one with their sense of their lives before them" (*BD* 139). In *The Child in Time*, Stephen refers to the inescapable task of positioning ourselves in moral space when he comments on his debate with an opponent of early literacy in his government committee. Thus, he claims: "It was that old business of [...] taking up a position, planting the flag of identity and self-esteem, then fighting all corners to the end" (*CT* 76). In Part Two of *Atonement* the symbol of the "map" alludes to the vital importance of mapping and orientation in our lives. Robbie Turner, released from prison to fight in the war, is in possession of a rear-area map of northern France (*A* 191), which - in the general chaos of the British army's retreat to Dunkirk in 1940 - directs him and the two corporals in his company to the safety of Bray Dunes (*A* 240). Urged on by a simple hypergood, "the small hard point of his own survival" (*A* 217), Robbie's task of mapping and orientation is reduced to the basics of pattern-building:

> [Y]ou walked across the land until you came to the sea. What could be simpler, once the social element was removed? He was the only man on earth and his purpose was clear. [...] The reality was all too social, he knew; other men were pursuing him, but he had comfort in a pretence, a rhythm at least for his feet. (*A* 219)

---

[184] Taylor, *Sources* 50.
[185] Taylor, *Sources* 41f.
[186] Taylor, *Sources* 29.

3.2 *Self* Among Other *Selves*: Autonomy versus Commitment

Despite their essentially private and inward concept of the *self*, the protagonists of *The Child in Time*, *Black Dogs*, *Enduring Love*, and *Atonement* are no isolated monads, shut off from others in their quest for the good life. They are *selves* among other *selves* as well as *selves* to them*selves*. As Booth puts it:

> [...] I embrace the pursuit of the Other as among the grandest of hunts we are invited to; from birth onward our growth depends so deeply on our ability to internalize other selves that one must be puzzled by those who talk about the self as somehow independent, individual, unsocial in this sense.[187]

McEwan's characters are involved in complex social interactions with other characters, incessantly trying to keep the balance between their sense of autonomy, individuality, and uniqueness and their commitment to the *selves* around them. In *Atonement*, thirteen-year-old Briony first becomes aware of the puzzling complexity of a world where individual selfhood is regarded as a property shared by all human beings:

> [T]he world, the social world, was unbearably complicated with two billion voices, and everyone's thoughts striving in equal importance and everyone's claim on life as intense, and everyone thinking they were unique, when no one was. One could drown in irrelevance. (*A* 36)

In a postmodern world, Herbert Grabes observes, "we have to reckon with a heightened degree of plurality, and that this likewise includes a high degree of heterogeneity, of alterity - not only in terms of coexistence or competition, but also of contradiction and conflict."[188]

Briony's despondent thoughts about the "irrelevance" of individual human existence in a world without inherent structures and full of contradictory thoughts striving in equal importance, mirror the confusion and disorientation characteristic of post-Enlightenment culture discussed in chapter one of this paper. With the birth of autonomous selfhood, Western culture erupted into a heterogeneous chorus of voices with no universally accepted master narrative to conduct them. Renouncing the concept of individual selfhood and embracing an "anything goes" attitude that (unsuccessfully) strives to sidestep a positioning of the *self* in moral space, however, is no solution to the struggle between autonomy and commitment, altruism and selfishness we are faced with in our

---
[187] Booth, *Company* 69.
[188] Herbert Grabes, "Ethics, Aesthetics, and Alterity," *Ethics and Aesthetics: The Moral Turn of Postmodernism*, ed. Gerhard Hoffmann and Alfred Hornung (Heidelberg: C. Winter, 1996) 19.

lives. Nor does it seem desirable or feasible to return to an essentialist version of the *self* and to try to avoid (moral) confusion by re-establishing categorical ethical precepts. The basic, irresolvable conflict between *self* and other, autonomy and commitment cannot be evaded, but must be individually coped with in our lives. Modern *self*-making, as Bruner puts it,

> [...] must on the one hand, create a conviction of autonomy, that one has a will of one's own, a certain freedom of choice, a degree of possibility. But it must also relate the self to a world of others [...]. We seem virtually unable to live without both, autonomy and commitment, and our lives strive to balance the two.[189]

The ballooning accident depicted in chapter one of *Enduring Love* constitutes a "test tube situation"[190] in the course of which the balancing activities needed to keep the diametrically opposed urges of altruism and selfishness in check are investigated under extreme but possible conditions. As McEwan states in an interview: "In it [the ballooning accident] I saw the parable, a microcosm, of one of those great conflicts in our lives between altruism and that other primary necessity of looking after yourself."[191] Joe and four other men are holding on to ropes attached to the helium balloon when it is lifted a few feet off the ground and one of the men jumps down. Joe claims that he does not know which of them let go first. He is deeply distressed by the knowledge that their collective weight would have brought the balloon safely back to the ground (*EL* 14). However, after the first person has broken ranks, the balloon surges upwards and hanging on becomes dangerous for the remaining men. Driven by the basic urge of *self*-preservation, they let go of the ropes one by one, leaving only John Logan to cling on for minute or so. When strength finally leaves Logan, he drops to the ground and dies.

In the aftermath of the fatal accident, Joe tries to analyse the catastrophe with the rational detachment of a scientist. He wonders if the dog-eat-dog mentality which manifested itself in the men's reaction after the first of them had jumped to the ground, was the dominant impulse inscribed in human nature. He knows that if the latter were the case, if there were nothing human beings could set against the overpowering instinct of their own survival and well-being, he would be released from all moral responsibility concerning the accident: "There was no team, there was no plan, no agreement to be broken. No failure.

---

[189] Bruner, *Making Stories* 78.
[190] In fact, Joe describes the minutes prior to the accident like the setting up of a scientific experiment: "[T]he convergence of six figures in a flat green space has a comforting geometry from the buzzard's perspective, the knowable, limited plane of the snooker table. The *initial conditions, the force and the direction of the force* define all the consequent pathways, all the angles of collision and return [...]. I think that while we were still converging, before we made contact, *we were in a state of mathematical grace* [emphases mine]" (*EL* 2).
[191] Schoeck, "Interview".

44

So can we accept that it was right, every man for himself? We were all happy afterwards that this was the reasonable course?" (*EL* 14). Still, Joe knows that the fully autonomous subject released from all social bounds does not exist, that

> [...] there was a deeper covenant, ancient and automatic, written in our nature. Co-operation – the basis of our earliest hunting successes, the force behind our evolving capacity for language, the glue of our social cohesion. Our misery in the aftermath was a proof that we knew we had failed ourselves. (*EL* 14)

Jeremy, rambling through the French countryside in *Black Dogs*, temporarily succumbs to the illusion that he is "self-sufficient and free, unencumbered by possessions and obligations" (*BD* 121), an autonomous subject, the creator of his own life, possessed of himself like the Nietzschean *Übermensch*. Thinking about "the whole pattern, the thumbnail story of [his] existence" (*BD* 122), he feels "balanced and purposeful" (*BD* 123), impervious to contingency and chaos, believing that nothing can unsettle his "schemes and projects" (*BD* 123). The unresolved cacophony of Bernard's and June's "indistinct voices" (*BD* 117) that troubled him the evening before has given way to a sense of control and sovereignty. Jeremy claims: "Rather than remain a passive victim of my subject's voices, I had come to pursue them, to re-create Bernard and June" (*BD* 122-123). Seeing himself as an active, autonomous *creator* rather than a heteronomous, passive *creature*, Jeremy is convinced that he can make his own meaning of the world, that he need neither submit to June's nor Bernard's, nor anyone else's interpretation of the universe. Metaphorically and literally, he takes a different path from the one Bernard and June took on their honeymoon in 1946: "That was their way, mine was different [...]; if I had to make a symbol of an overgrown path, this would suit me better" (*BD* 123). In fact, *Black Dogs* could have ended at this point, with Jeremy "taking control" (*BD* 123) of his life and finally renouncing his substitute parents whose "spiritual" guidance, he had hoped, could provide an epistemological hearth.

However, later that day, Jeremy dines in a hôtel-restaurant where he witnesses a French father brutally beat his young son. The loneliness and helplessness of the child in the face of "the unrestrained force of adult hatred" (*BD* 129) reminds Jeremy of the loneliness he and his niece Sally experienced in their childhood, he as an orphan, she as the daughter of a chain smoking "Jean Harlow look-alike" (*BD* 13) and a "sadistic [...] leather feticheur" (*BD* 13). Spurred on by an "ennobling sense" (*BD* 130) of justice and revenge, Jeremy beats up the boy's father, claiming: "[I]t was a drama that seemed to be enacted for me alone. [...] It represented a purging, an exorcism, in which I acted on behalf of my niece Sally, as well as for myself, and took our revenge" (*BD* 124). Jeremy only refrains from kicking the man to death when another guest calls him back with the exactly the same words June used to address the fierce black dogs approaching her on a coastal path during her honeymoon: "Ça suffit!" (*BD*

124, 131, 149). Immediately, Jeremy knows "that the elation driving [him] had nothing to do with revenge and justice" (*BD* 131), that his violent reaction to the father's violence was not the heroic act of an autonomous subject in control of his own life, but a manifestation of uncontrollable animal energy (*BD* 131). As Pedot remarks:

> Jeremy [...] devient le sujet, au sens passif, de son propre récit. [...] Le retour inopiné de la voix de June, derrière celle de la cliente de l'hôtel institue Jeremy, en tant que chien noir, en sujet du récit, mais le destitue par là même de sa position de sujet maître de la narration.[192]

Jeremy realises that *self*-creation is not the fully autonomous act he believed it to be only a few hours earlier, but that, as a *self*, he is "a focal point in a field of forces",[193] continually torn between autonomy and heteronomy.[194] *Self*-creation, Derek Attridge asserts, "is both an act and an event, both something that is done and something that happens."[195] Similarly, MacIntyre claims that "we are never more (and sometimes less) than the co-authors of our own narrative. Only in fantasy do we live the story we please."[196] As social animals "[w]e enter upon a stage which we did not design and we find ourselves part of an action that was not of our making."[197]

In *Atonement*, thirteen-year-old Briony becomes aware of this simple truth while chopping nettles with a stick near the island temple of the Tallises' estate, picturing herself as a unique, pre-eminent master in the newly devised "field of nettle slashing" (*A* 76), certain to win gold for England in the Berlin Olympics of the following year (*A* 75). Once her childish reveries have given way to reality, Briony loses "her godly power of creation" (*A* 76), becoming yet again "a solitary girl swiping nettles with a stick" (*A* 76). Musing about this transformation, Briony comes to the conclusion: "But of course, it had all been about her – by her and about her, and now *she was back in the world, not one she could make, but one that had made her* [emphasis mine]" (*A* 76). Discussing *Atonement* in an interview, McEwan explains that one of his motivations for writing the novel has been an interest in "examin[ing] the relationship between

---

[192] Pedot, "Narration" 73.
[193] Booth, *Company* 239f.
[194] Note that Jeremy's realisation that he cannot create the narrative of his life as a fully autonomous subject mirrors the insight Robbie Turner gains during his retreat to Dunkirk: "Long ago, before the war, before Wandsworth, he used to revel in his freedom to make his own life, devise his own story with only the distant help of Jack Tallis. Now he understood how conceited that delusion was. Rootless, therefore futile" (*A* 241).
[195] Derek Attridge, "Innovation, Literature, Ethics: Relating to the Other," *PMLA* 114 (1999): 22.
[196] MacIntyre, *After Virtue* 199.
[197] MacIntyre, *After Virtue* 199.

what is imagined and what is true", declaring himself intrigued with "the danger of an imagination that can't quite see the boundaries of what is real and what is unreal."[198]

Briony, a girl "possessed by the desire to have the world just so" (*A* 4), has to painfully learn that she is no autonomous Author-God in a world as neatly structured as her plays, where "a love of order shaped the principles of justice" (*A* 7), where all fates are resolved (*A* 6) and where "her passion for tidiness" (*A* 7) is always satisfied. Although it deeply upsets her "controlling demon" (*A* 5) and her "wish for a harmonious, organised world" (*A* 5), Briony realises that reality does not follow the dictates of her imagination, but contains other *selves* with needs just like her own:

> The self-contained world she had drawn with clear and perfect lines had been defaced with the scribble of other minds, other needs; and time itself, so easily sectioned on paper into acts and scenes, was even now dribbling uncontrollably away. (*A* 36 – 37)

However, only a few hours later, Briony falls victim to her overactive imagination and her passion for excessive pattern-building when she chances upon Lola lying on the ground near the island temple immediately after the rape. Having (mis)read an explicit sexual note written by Robbie and sent by mistake to Cecilia, having stumbled upon Robbie and her sister making love in the manor's library earlier the same day and misinterpreting the scene as an attack on her sister, Briony is convinced that Robbie is "a villain in the form of an old family friend" (*A* 158). She files him away as a stock character of gothic literature, "the incarnation of evil" (*A* 115), and hence the only person who could have attacked her cousin in the dark. Briony claims: "[T]he affair was too consistent, too symmetrical to be anything other than what she said it was" (*A* 168). Thus, although she did not actually see Robbie turn away from Lola's huddled shape, she convinces herself that Robbie is the figure she glimpsed running away from her cousin in the dark. Briony is unwilling or unable to concede that reality does not always fit in with her desire for a consistent, logically structured, symmetrical universe, that she has misunderstood what she has seen, read, and heard during the day, and that there are stories apart from her own claiming to be heard. A thoroughly *self*-centred pattern-builder, Briony insists that "[e]verything connected. It was *her own* discovery. It was *her* story, the one that was writing itself around *her* [emphases mine]" (*A* 166).

In *The Child in Time*, Charles Drake, former senior editor of a famous literary publisher, up-and-coming government minister, and protégé of the Prime Minister, succumbs to a story of the *self* that violates the boundaries of what is real and what is unreal. He dons boys' clothes, adopts the habits of a ten-year-old, and spends his days in a tree-house (*CT* 106). Charles Drake's

---

[198] Reynolds and Noakes, *Ian McEwan* 19.

regression into childhood can be regarded as an extreme attempt to avoid the inescapable struggle between private autonomy and public commitment that we are faced with as adult members of society. By escaping into a "real" fantasy world of childhood Charles relinquishes his adult responsibilities and ceases to be an answerable player in the balancing game between *self* and other. As Charles's wife Thelma puts it:

> He wanted the security of childhood, the powerlessness, the obedience, and also the freedom that goes with it, freedom from money, decisions, plans, demands. [...] Childhood for him was timeless, he talked about it as though it were a mystical state. (*CT* 202)

However, Charles's *self*-sufficient mystical state does not endure. Torn between the ambition to succeed in the harsh public world of politics and the desire to maintain his innocence as a careless boy (*CT* 201), he commits suicide. His schizophrenic state of mind is reflected in the secretly-published, harsh-voiced, authoritarian "Childcare manual" (*CT* 202) of which he turns out to be the author. Thelma tells Stephen that the manual is "a perfect illustration of Charles's problem. It was his fantasy life which drew him to the work, and it was his desire to please the boss which made him write it the way he did. That's what he couldn't square, and that's why he fell apart" (*CT* 205). Thelma regards her husband's inability to keep the balance between the public and the private aspects of selfhood, between autonomy and commitment, as "an extreme form of a general problem" (*CT* 205) we are confronted with as human beings. Similarly, Rorty points out that although, as post-Enlightenment moderns, we have freed ourselves "gradually but steadily, from theology and metaphysics" and have substituted "Freedom for Truth as the goal of thinking and of social progress [...], the old tension between the private and the public remains."[199]

---

[199] Rorty, *Contingency* xiii.

4. Taking Perspectives: Stories of the *Self*

4.1 The Poly-Storied *Self*: Selfhood and Cultural Tradition

We suggested in the preceding chapter that the modern notion of the fully autonomous *self*, "[picturing] the human person as, at least potentially, finding its own bearings within, declaring independence from the webs of interlocution which have originally formed him/her",[200] does not exist. We argued that as *selves*, we are immersed in a community with other *selves*, continuously balancing our ineradicable sense of autonomy, individuality, and inwardness with our commitment to what Seyla Benhabib calls "concrete others",[201] i.e. *selves* like ourselves with "a certain life history, disposition and endowment, as well as needs and limitations."[202] Throughout our lives we arbitrate between the inescapable task of taking a position in moral space "that is inextricably linked to our subjectivity"[203] and the inevitable necessity to do so in the public realm of concrete others. In fact, we find our "moral identity in and through its membership in communities such as those of the family, the neighbourhood, the city and the tribe."[204] As Taylor claims: "The full definition of someone's identity [...] involves not only his stand on moral and spiritual matters but also a reference to a defining community."[205] Taking a stand in moral space implies taking a perspective on the world that is uniquely ours. However, until we can interpret others as having a perspective on things just like our*selves*, there is no room for the idea of our having a perspective. Indeed, the very notion of perspective that belongs to the concept of *self* "depend[s] on our ability to see ourselves as a person in a world of persons."[206]

Still, as *selves*, we are not only bound to and influenced by the contemporary members of our defining communities, but we find ourselves part of a particular cultural history, "a specific past that is present to some degree in [our] present."[207] Our individual *self*-narratives are integrated into the unfolding narrative of our cultural community, its past, present, and virtual future. So, for instance, in *The Child in Time*, young Stephen regards himself as "a potential Joyce, Mann or Shakespeare" belonging "without question to the European

---

[200] Taylor, *Sources* 36.
[201] Benhabib, *Situating* 10.
[202] Benhabib, *Situating* 10.
[203] Antor, "Ethics" 76.
[204] MacIntyre, *After Virtue* 205.
[205] Taylor, *Sources* 36.
[206] J.D.D. Hutto, "The Story of the Self: The Narrative Basis of Self-Development," *Ethics and the Subject*, ed. Karl Simms (Amsterdam: Rodopi, 1997) 75.
[207] MacIntyre, *After Virtue* 206.

tradition" (*CT* 25) and Jeremy in *Black Dogs* borrows phrases from Kafka (*BD* 15), Sylvia Plath (*BD* 18), and Proust "to announce [himself] to the world as an intellectual" (*BD* 14) of European provenance. MacIntyre postulates that the living tradition of a community "is an historically extended, socially embodied argument, and an argument precisely in part about the goods which constitute that tradition."[208] As human beings, we live with a stock of conflicting and complementary narratives accumulated over the centuries and, "[j]ust as our opposable forefingers and thumbs enable us to use many tools, our narrative gift gives us access to the culture's treasury of stories."[209]

Living with the past of a specific cultural community, its (conflicting) values and versions of the good life, however, does not imply that we are slaves to our respective cultures. In fact, "[w]e nourish our identities by our connections yet insist that we are something more as well – ourselves."[210] We are, as Bruner elaborates, free to choose among a great variety of possible, heterogeneous models of selfhood based on certain "presuppositions and perspectives about selfhood, rather like plot summaries or homilies for telling oneself or others about oneself."[211] Human life, Booth observes in a similar fashion, is "inherently, inescapably multivalent, poly-storied, pluri-mythic."[212] Creating our*selves*, "we are beneficiaries of our culture's ongoing dialectic."[213] We draw on the rich resources of our cultural heritage - its myths, narratives, explanatory patterns - to invest our lives with meaning, to define our position in moral space, and to deal with the other in day-to-day living. As *bricoleurs*, or improvisers,[214] we patch together our individual *self*-narratives from a great variety of different stories based on a whole range of "moral sources"[215] and "paradigms of knowledge"[216] provided by science, art, religion, and philosophy. As Lay Clayton puts it: The *self* "tells a story of unitary experience producing a single stream through the multiple possibilities of the world."[217]

In chapter four of this paper we will investigate how the protagonists of *The Child in Time, Black Dogs, Enduring Love*, and *Atonement* make use of the moral sources, stories, or explanatory patterns supplied by science, religion, and

---

[208] MacIntyre, *After Virtue* 207.
[209] Bruner, *Making Stories* 100.
[210] Bruner, *Making Stories* 100.
[211] Bruner, *Making Stories* 66.
[212] Booth, *Company* 348.
[213] Bruner, *Making Stories* 100.
[214] Bruner, *Making Stories* 100.
[215] Taylor, *Sources* 91ff.
[216] Patricia Waugh, "Revising the Two Cultures Debate: Science, Literature and Value," David Fuller and Patricia Waugh, *The Arts and Sciences of Criticism* (Oxford: Oxford UP, 1999) 33.
[217] Lay Clayton, "The absent signifier: historical narrative and the abstract subject," *Ethics and the Subject*, ed. Karl Simms (Amsterdam: Rodopi, 1997) 79.

literature. We will analyse how McEwan's characters articulate the good in their lives, position themselves in moral space, and invest their lives with meaning. In short, we will examine their individual perspectives on a world in which a confusing number of conflicting explanatory patterns is abroad.

4.2 The Two Cultures Debate: Science versus Literature

As Patricia Waugh states, "every culture has witnessed struggles for dominance between rival paradigms of knowledge which have also been struggles to establish a structure of values [...]."[218] The struggle between the epistemologies or value systems of science and literature[219] can be traced back to Antiquity, where "an emergent ideal of rationalism vie[d] with a literary culture concerned with the training of the orator lawyer."[220] In the seventeenth century, intellectual achievements such as the scientific discoveries of Sir Isaac Newton, the rationalism of Descartes, and the empiricism of Francis Bacon and John Locke smoothed the way for a culture exulting in reason and scientific methods. However, after the bloody Revolution of 1789 and with the beginning of industrialisation, old rules and certainties were threatened. The "enlightened" ambition and optimism to fully understand the world and create a just and equal society turned into terror and disillusion.[221] Where once it seemed possible to reason one's way to a better world, and knowledge of the whole Truth of the universe seemed within reach, now many feared that human beings were unfathomably dark, irrational, and lost creatures. As the dominant aesthetic movement of late eighteenth and early nineteenth century, Romanticism turned to the creation of shared value (the beautiful) and tried to substitute an intuition of worlds beyond the actual (the sublime) for universal Truth and cognitive certainty.[222]

From the eighteenth century onwards the struggle of dominance between the realms of science and literature "has tended to proceed with a culture of letters defending the value of a conceptually indefinable form of knowledge"[223]

---

[218] Waugh, "Revising" 33.
[219] Note that in the dichotomy between science and literature, 'science' denotes a whole range of disciplines and subdisciplines, across the range of chemistry, medicine, biology, and physics. 'Literature' is promoted from the level of an individual discipline to a broad umbrella term; in fact, it has been "constructed within the literature-science debate as a paradigmatic humanities subject" (Daniel Cordle, *Postmodern Postures: Literature, Science and the Two Cultures Debate*. Aldershot: Ashgate, 1999. 13).
[220] Waugh, "Revising" 33.
[221] Cf. Paul Langford, "The Eighteenth Century," *The Oxford History of Britain*, ed. Kenneth O. Morgan (1983; Oxford: Oxford UP, 1993) 399ff.
[222] Aidan Day, *Romanticism* (London: Routledge, 1996) 64f.
[223] Waugh, "Revising" 35.

against empirical science claiming to offer "'hard', 'objective' truth: truth as correspondence to reality, the only sort of truth worthy of the name."[224] The famous "two cultures debate" between C.P. Snow and F.R. Leavis in 1959[225] represented "the tail-end of a 200-year-old version of the ancient debate about exact and inexact kinds of knowledge which was about to be radically challenged by developments in both cultures."[226] In the second half of the twentieth century, the two cultures divide between science and literature narrowed with the realisation that there exists no objective, exact, or final way of approaching reality, and that in the sciences as well as the arts, "truth is made rather than found."[227]

In *The Child in Time* and *Enduring Love*, Ian McEwan enters into the two cultures debate by making his main characters representatives and defenders of either the science or the literature side of the struggle. Stephen in the *Child in Time* is a writer of children's literature and Thelma a theoretical physicist, a teacher of science, and an expounder of scientific ideas. Joe in *Enduring Love* is a writer on science and a fervent advocate of rationalism and materialism whereas his partner Clarissa studies and teaches Romantic poetry. *Atonement* constitutes a departure from McEwan's earlier work insofar as the dialogue between the epistemologies of science and literature, which pervades the thematic structure of *The Child in Time* and *Enduring Love*, is of no central thematic interest in the novel. However, McEwan's "twin hunger"[228] for the explanatory patterns of science and literature resurfaces in chapter eight of Part One of *Atonement* where Robbie Turner, having taken a degree in English literature at Cambridge, decides to study medicine to further his education.

In *The Child in Time*, the two cultures debate centres on the confrontation between Stephen's artistic imagination and the theories advanced by modern science. Thelma Drake, retired from active teaching and research, is writing a synthesis of modern science in which she undertakes to highlight the impact of scientific revolutions such as relativity, quantum theory, and backward flowing

---

[224] Rorty, *Objectivity* 35.
[225] When C.P Snow delivered his 1959 Rede lecture in Cambridge he put forward a by then already outdated model of empirical science, claiming that "the external world [can] be accurately and exhaustively described, its facts captured in transparent propositions which are the truths of its discoveries. [...] Complacently secure in the 'exactness' of his professed discipline [...], Snow [launched] his attack on the narcissistic, 'feline and oblique' culture of modern letters" (Waugh, "Revising" 37f). F.R. Leavis defended literary culture "in the now familiar terms of the 'value' of a kind of knowledge which is strictly indefinable, which cannot be adequately discussed because it only exists as a [cultural] practice" (Waugh, "Revising" 37).
[226] Waugh, "Revising" 36.
[227] Rorty, *Contingency* 7.
[228] Garner, "Salon Interview".

time (*CT* 39) on various fields and aspects of human life. Outlining parts of her book to Stephen, Thelma explains:

> Think how humanised and approachable scientists would be if they could join in the really important conversations about time, and without thinking they had the final word - the mystic's experience of timelessness, the chaotic unfolding time in dreams, the Christian moment of fulfilment and redemption, the annihilated time of deep sleep, the elaborate time schemes of novelists, poets, daydreamers, the infinite, unchanging time of childhood. (*CT* 118)

Modern physicists can no longer lay claim to the objectivity of their research, or as Thelma puts it: "The measurers of the world can no longer detach themselves. They have to measure themselves too" (*CT* 40). Thelma believes that science is growing up and becoming more feminine,[229] ready to accommodate anti-Newtonian concepts and prepared to avow that our everyday experiences of time, space, and matter are nothing but "intricate illusions" (*CT* 40).

A representative of the science side of the two cultures debate Thelma accuses "'arts' people" (*CT* 40) of being unmoved and ignorant in the presence of quantum physics which to her is nothing short of "[a] scientific revolution, no, an intellectual revolution, an emotional, sensual explosion, a fabulous story just beginning to unfold" (*CT* 40). Thelma explains to Stephen how theoretical physics - with its vast potential of possibilities - could have influenced literature:

> Shakespeare would have grasped wave functions, Donne would have understood complementarity and relative time. They would have been excited. What richness! They would have plundered new science for their imagery. And they would have educated their audiences too. But you "arts" people, you are not only ignorant of these magnificent things, you're rather proud of knowing nothing. (*CT* 40)

Thelma concludes her harangue against "'arts' people", railing against the lack of diachronic progress and accumulative knowledge in literary studies: "As far as you can make out, you think that some local, passing fashion like modernism - modernism! - is the intellectual achievement of our time. Pathetic!" (*CT* 40).[230]

---

[229] Thelma claims that quantum mechanics will "feminise physics, all science, make it softer, less arrogantly detached, more receptive to participating in the world it wanted to describe" (*CT* 39). In contrast to "the 'masculine' Old Physics [which is] presented as impartial, exclusive, deterministic, presumptuously knowing, and single-minded [...], the 'feminine' New Physics is participatory, self-inclusive, choice-oriented, humbly agnostic, and multiple in perspective" (Wright, "Physics" 225).

[230] Thelma does not consider that modernist literature sought to integrate the discoveries of modern science into its writing. Influenced by Einstein's relativity theory and Heisenberg's indeterminacy, modernist fiction took part in a radical modern departure, across all of the arts, from realism and verisimilitude. Paul Edwards, "Time, Romanticism, Modernism and Moderation in Ian McEwan's *The Child in Time*," *English* 44 (1995): 44ff.

Stephen is deeply impressed by the unexpected "poignant complex of hope and [...] consolation"[231] that Thelma's account of backward flowing time and parallel universes opens up to him. He believes that her "quantum magic" (*CT* 39) will redeem, diminish, or evade the loss of his daughter and help him reconnect to some meaningful concept of the *self* and the universe. Thus, on the one hand, Stephen makes use of the theory of backward flowing time to mentally re-enter the moment before Kate is abducted, constructing alternative stories in which he is able to lift his eyes "against the weight of time" (*CT* 10), see the abductor and save his daughter. On the other hand, he falls back upon the multiple universe theory of the quantum to comfort himself with the thought "that his daughter, though absent from his own world, continues to exist and grow older in another, numinous dimension."[232] For the major part of the novel, Stephen likes to think of himself as "the father of an invisible child" (*CT* 2) whose "phantom growth" (*CT* 2) in a parallel universe induces him to keep on the look-out for children whose features resemble his daughter's. By searching for traces of Kate in a beggar girl (*CT* 2-3) and a schoolgirl in the playground of a primary school (*CT* 141), Stephen endeavours "to give substance to [Kate's] continued existence" (*CT* 2) and keep her alive in his hopes.

However, when the headmaster of the primary school convinces him that the girl he took for Kate cannot possibly be his lost daughter (*CT* 150), Stephen reluctantly concedes that "there were many paths Kate might have gone down, countless ways in which she might have changed in two and a half years and that he knew nothing about any of them" (*CT* 152). In fact, Kate never returns in the novel, she remains a "lost, irreplaceable child" (*CT* 217) about whose whereabouts, abductor, or murderer we are left totally in the dark. Hence, in the end, Thelma's quantum magic fails to come off for Stephen; the explanatory patterns provided by new physics turn out to be irrelevant in the process of accepting and overcoming the loss of his daughter. The simple, idealised transference of the quantum into the realm of artistic imagination proves futile, illusory and, in Stephen's case, even counter-productive: The faith in Thelma's quantum magic keeps him running after his daughter in his mind, believing her to grow older in some parallel universe to which he is denied access. As Derek Wright sums up:

> *The Child in Time* is a [...] record of the doomed attempts of the dreaming artistic imagination [...] to translate the abstruse theoretical concepts of the New Physics across the culture gap into everyday phenomenal experience: to bring the quantum into quotidian reality.[233]

---

[231] Wright, "Physics" 226.
[232] Wright, "Physics" 226f.
[233] Wright, "Physics" 223.

Joe Rose in *Enduring Love* prides himself on being a materialist, a rationalist with "a talent for clarity" (*EL* 75), and an empiricist viewing the world through the prism of physical data. Passing the ballooning accident in review, for example, Joe assesses the percentage gradient of the sloping ground over which the balloon hangs (*EL* 10) and calculates the mathematics of the failed rescue attempt, claiming that "if we had assumed an average weight of a hundred and sixty pounds each, then surely eight hundred pounds would have kept us close to the ground" (*EL* 55). Joe believes that the vocabulary of science puts him "in touch with how things *really* are, in a way that contrasts invidiously with the sort of 'contact with reality' provided by other vocabularies";[234] vocabularies such as the "unreasonable" (*EL* 222), "clammy emotional" (*EL* 222) vocabulary of literature favoured by his partner Clarissa.[235]

Fascinated by the literary movement of Romanticism, Clarissa[236] takes a subjective, emotional, imaginative approach to her surroundings, an approach diametrically opposed to Joe's "enlightened" ambition to rationalise the world and to objectively, scientifically label its components. Joe is convinced that Clarissa spends too much time in the company of John Keats, "[a] genius no doubt", he concedes, "but an obscurantist too who had thought science was robbing the world of wonder, when the opposite was the case" (*EL* 71). Joe is, in fact, a defender of a radical scientism which "[takes] the practical success of science as reason to understand its vocabulary as putting us in closer touch with reality than others."[237] Joe's world-view is characterised by an almost snobbish belief in the epistemological superiority of his chosen domain. He complains, for instance, about the "derisory" (*EL* 42) science collection of the London Library with words that call to mind Thelma's invective against modernism in *The Child in Time*:

> The assumption appeared to be that the world could be sufficiently understood through fictions, histories and biographies. Did the scientific illiterates who ran this place, and who dared call themselves educated people, really believe that literature was the greatest intellectual achievement of our civilization? (*EL* 42)

---

[234] Robert Brandom, ed., introduction, *Rorty and His Critics* (Malden, Mass.: Blackwell, 2000) v.

[235] Throughout the novel, Joe's vocabulary is characterised by a high degree of scientific exactitude. So, for instance, Joe describes his actions and feelings during the ballooning accident with words like "barely a neuronal impulse later" (*EL* 13), and "thoughts in which fear and instant calculations of logarithmic complexity were fused" (*EL* 13).

[236] Note in this context that Clarissa's name echoes that of the eponymous heroine of Samuel Richardson's novel *Clarissa* (1748) and thus - though not referring to the period of Romanticism - has strong literary connotations.

[237] Brandom, *Rorty and His Critics* xiv.

The picture Joe paints of himself appears foursquare and solid - a rationalist, a materialist, a man of science who speaks with confidence and utmost certainty about himself, other people, and the world he inhabits. For example, about the ballooning accident Joe says: "I know if I had been the uncontested leader the tragedy would not have happened" (*EL* 11). After a quarrel with Clarissa, in which she tried to persuade Joe that Jed Parry is "a pathetic and harmless crank" (*EL* 216), hinting even that he might be nothing but a creature of Joe's imagination (*EL* 216), Joe wants to make it up with her "not because [he] had behaved badly or was wrong, but because [he] was so obviously, incontrovertibly right, and she was simply mistaken" (*EL* 92). When a diner sitting at a table next to him and Clarissa in a restaurant is shot at, Joe is firmly convinced that the shooting is a miscarried attempt on his own life by a couple of hit-men hired by Parry. Joe tells the police:

> I might as well tell you straight away that *I know what happened* [emphasis mine]. The bullet that hit Mr Tapp was meant for me. The man who was eating alone and who intervened is someone who's been bothering me. His name is Parry. (*EL* 175-176)

When neither the police nor Clarissa believe his account of the shooting, Joe decides to purchase a gun and, if necessary, confront Parry single-handedly. Joe's increasing panic, the absence of evidence that Parry actually *was* in the restaurant when Tapp is shot,[238] and his open avowal that "[b]elieving is seeing" (*EL* 181) impair his status as a reliable, objective, matter-of-fact narrator. As readers, we become aware of the fact that we have only Joe's word that Parry is obsessively in love with him and that the harassment is serious. In fact, we begin to suspect that Joe might be suffering from groundless persecution mania. For a while, Timothy Bewes points out, the text remains in an interesting state of ambiguity: "[W]ho is mad, Joe or Jed? The rationalist or the religious believer? Alternatively, who has the correct analysis of Jed's behaviour, Joe or Clarissa? The scientist or the literary scholar?"[239] As McEwan explains in an interview: "I wanted the reader to toy with the idea that Joe is going completely crazy, or maybe even that Joe was Jed."[240]

It turns out, however, that sober, rational Joe has been right about Parry's condition, his presence in the restaurant, and the danger he constitutes in his delusional state when Parry takes Clarissa hostage, holding her at knife-point,

---

[238] Joe claims that Parry tried to prevent the hired assassins from killing Tapp. As Parry has cut off his trademark pony-tail, Joe does not recognise him straight away (*EL* 173). Clarissa, however, who knows Parry from the scene of the ballooning accident, does not recognise Parry at all.
[239] Timothy Bewes, "What is Philosophical Honesty in Postmodern Literature?" *New Literary History* 31 (2000): 430.
[240] Reynolds and Noakes, *Ian McEwan* 17.

paradoxically, to obtain Joe's forgiveness for having attempted to murder him in the restaurant the day before. Further overwhelming evidence of Parry's insanity is provided in the form of the article on de Clérambault's syndrome in appendix I. The latter contains a case-study of one de Clérambault's sufferer P. whose medical history closely resembles Joe's narrative portrayal of Parry in the novel. The spoof article,[241] in combination with another apparently authentic letter in appendix II, written by Parry from the confines of a mental hospital, leads Bewes to conclude that the novel closes with "an overwhelming endorsement of Joe's scientific rationalism against both Jed's fanaticism and Clarissa's sympathetic literary sensitivity."[242]

Are the ambiguities of *Enduring Love* really as neatly and convincingly cleared up as Bewes maintains? Is Joe's rationalism, objectivism, and scientific superiority really "left almost entirely unquestioned, unimpaired, by the narrative [...]"?[243] In fact, although Joe correctly classifies Parry as a de Clérambault's sufferer whose delusions can take a violent turn, Joe's status as an advocate of scientific rationalism is compromised fairly early in the novel. We learn that Joe is no research scientist (*EL* 38), but only a mediator of science who makes intelligible to the layperson the world of scientific discovery as "a journalist, a commentator, an outsider to [his] own profession" (*EL* 77). Indeed, far from being the pure-blood rationalist, objectivist, and materialist he claims to be, Joe represents a modified form of scientific rationalism in its pure state. His ideas and theories are already once removed from the originally researched "truth" of science. As Joe puts it himself:

> [A]ll the ideas I deal in are other people's. I simply collate and digest their research, and deliver it up to the general reader [...]. In my bad moments the thought returns that I'm a parasite [...]. (*EL* 75)

Thus, Joe turns out to be an unreliable representative of the very world-view he advocates; he is a pariah in the world of research science, convinced that "no scientist, not even a lab technician or college porter" (*EL* 77) would take him seriously.

As a popular scientist - i.e. someone who can "spin a decent narrative out of the stumblings, back-trackings and random successes that lie behind most scientific research" (*EL* 75) - Joe is closer to the subjective world of fiction than

---

[241] Although Ian McEwan made up the article on Parry's medical condition, de Clérambault's syndrome is authentic: "Gaetan de Clérambault (1872-1934) was a celebrated Parisian psychiatrist who described behaviour that bears a close resemblance to that depicted in McEwan's novel" (Malcolm, *Understanding* 204).
[242] Malcolm, *Understanding* 430.
[243] Bewes, "Philosophical Honesty" 430.

he dares to admit. Re-reading his article on "the death of the anecdote and narrative in science" (*EL* 41)[244] he comes to the shattering conclusion:

> What I had written wasn't true. It wasn't written in the pursuit of truth, it wasn't science. It was journalism, whose ultimate standard was readability […]. I could make a separate coherent piece out of the counter arguments (the twentieth century saw the summation of narrative science etc.). (*EL* 50-51)

Joe does not realise, however, that making coherent pieces out of counter arguments is no procedure restricted to the realms of journalism or literature, but that our perspectives on the world are always open to redescriptions and counter-arguments, in the sciences as well as the humanities. In fact, as Rorty points out, "anything [can] be made to look good or bad, important or unimportant, useful or useless, by being redescribed."[245] Trying to stick as closely as possible to his scientific model of reality, Joe misses out on other, equally coherent ways of (re)describing the world. As McEwan states in an interview: "There is something about Clarissa's take on the world that Joe badly needs. But I wrote the book in a spirit of investigation, rather than trying to give a lot of answers to either how people should live or whether one could live a good life by a scientific method."[246]

In *Atonement*, McEwan has Robbie Turner take up the two cultures debate between science and literature, offering yet another antirepresentationalist account of the two epistemological frameworks. Recently graduated from Cambridge with a degree in English literature, Robbie suffers a kind of epistemological crisis:

> Despite his first, the study of English seemed in retrospect an absorbing parlour game, and reading books and having opinions about them, the desirable adjunct to a civilised existence. But it was not the core, whatever Dr Leavis said in his lectures. It was not the necessary priesthood, nor the most vital pursuit of an enquiring mind, nor the first and the last defence against a barbarian horde, any more than the study of music, history or science. (*A* 91)

Robbie realises that no framework of belief "can be taken for granted as *the* framework tout court, can sink to the phenomenological status of unquestioned

---

[244] Joe's article is concerned with the overlapping between the realms of science and literature. Proof-reading his piece, Joe realises that the boundaries between science and literature in the twentieth century are by no means as clearly drawn as he claims in his article: "[W]hat of those behaviourists and sociologists of the nineteen twenties? It was as though an army of white-coated Balzacs had stormed the university departments and labs" (*EL* 50).
[245] Rorty, *Contingency* 7.
[246] Garner, "Salon Interview".

fact"[247] and offer a quasi-divine, infallible interpretation of reality. Like Joe in *Enduring Love* - who is unsettled by the awareness that he can make a separate coherent piece out of the counter arguments for his article on the "anecdotal scientist" (*EL* 41) - Robbie is disconcerted by the insight that different, incommensurable frameworks of belief can be defended with equal logic and coherence:

> At various talks in his final year Robbie had heard a psychoanalyst, a Communist trade union official and a physicist each declare for his own field as passionately, as convincingly, as Leavis had for his own. Such claims were probably made for medicine [...]. (*A* 91)

Robbie knows, that despite the absence of a universally accepted master version of truth or reality, he has to take a stand in moral space and orientate himself towards some good. The knowledge acquired in the study of English literature, however, does no longer satisfy his intellectual curiosity; he is conscious of the need - both literally and metaphorically - to travel, i.e. to change and thereby widen his conceptual horizon.[248] Longing for an occupation that brings him into closer contact with the practical aspects of everyday life than the isolated study of literary texts advocated by F.R. Leavis and I.A. Richards,[249] Robbie turns to medicine, probably the most practically-minded and human-centred of the sciences. The prospect of studying medicine in Edinburgh fills him with a sense of freedom, purpose, and new beginnings:

> [H]is practical nature and his frustrated scientific aspirations would find an outlet, he would have skills far more elaborate than the ones he had acquired in practical criticism, and above all he would have made his own decision. He would take lodgings in a strange town – and begin. (*A* 91)

However, Robbie does not intend to abandon literature completely. Rather, he endeavours to bridge the two cultures gap reinforced by his teacher Leavis who - throughout his career - doggedly refused to regard science as a cultural achievement and strove to set up his own discipline as a cultural master narrative, claiming "that literature could save us, and even that *only* literature could save us."[250] Robbie believes that the ethical knowledge and imaginative power acquired in three years of literary studies will usefully supplement his

---

[247] Taylor, *Sources* 17.
[248] Cf. Antor, "Ethics" 72.
[249] "Practical criticism" as pioneered by I.A. Richards in his study *Practical Criticism: A Study of Literary Judgement* (1929) is "based on [the] close analysis of a text in isolation" (Cuddon, *Dictionary* 738). Interpreting texts, students are asked to attend to the words on the page rather than refer to biographical and historical contexts.
[250] Cordner, "F.R. Leavis" 81.

medical skills. In fact, he is convinced that "he would be a better doctor for having read literature" (*A* 93). In other words, Robbie endeavours to combine the vocabulary of literary analysis with the vocabulary of science to create a new vocabulary which he hopes will enable him to read a deeper meaning into the rise and fall of human existence (*A* 93) and thus reveal a coherent picture behind the partial views gained by the solitary study of science or literature. Robbie's idealistic concept of a marriage between the "two cultures" is greatly indebted to nineteenth-century fiction, "which constantly modelled itself, whether literally or metaphorically, on science"[251] and of which Zola's naturalism, theorised in *The Experimental Novel* (1880), was the culminating example. Thus, Robbie day-dreams:

> What deep readings his modified sensibility might make of human suffering, of the self-destructive folly or sheer bad luck that drive men towards ill-health! Birth, death, and frailty in between. Rise and fall – this was the doctor's business, and it was literature's too. He was thinking of the nineteenth-century novel. Broad tolerance and a long view, an inconspicuously warm heart and cool judgement; his kind of doctor would be alive to the monstrous patterns of fate, and the vain and comical denial of the inevitable; he would press the enfeebled pulse, hear the expiring breath, feel the fevered hand begin to cool and reflect, in a manner that only literature and religion teach, on the puniness and nobility of mankind. (*A* 93)[252]

The creation of a new vocabulary, however, is not a discovery about how old vocabularies fit together like pieces of a jigsaw-puzzle to form a coherent, pre-ordained whole.[253] Robbie's combined vocabulary of medicine and literary analysis does not lead to a "discovery [...] of a reality behind the appearances, of an undistorted view of the whole picture with which to replace myopic views of its parts."[254] We observed earlier in this paper that there is no single vocabulary that puts us in contact with *the* true, intrinsic nature of either the *self* or the world. We can now add to this proposition that there is just as little ground for believing that a combination of two or more different vocabularies will achieve this objective. In fact, each newly devised vocabulary or tool in the language game merely constitutes a further perspective on a world where meaning is made rather than found.[255]

---

[251] Michael Bell, "The Metaphysics of Modernism," *The Cambridge Companion to Modernism*, ed. Michael Levenson (Cambridge: Cambridge UP, 1999) 11.
[252] Note that, ironically, Robbie's medical ambitions are thwarted by the misguided influence of the very literature he claims will make him a better doctor. When Briony's literary imagination runs riot, Robbie becomes the victim of the young girl's literary misinterpretation, her all too "deep readings" of the people and events surrounding her.
[253] Rorty, *Contingency* 12.
[254] Rorty, *Contingency* 12.
[255] Rorty, *Contingency* 13.

Indeed, the two cultures conflict is not neatly resolved in Ian McEwan's novels. Neither science nor literature hold a universal epistemological key to the world or the good life, nor does an idealistic marriage of the two cultural paradigms offer an unambiguous answer to the Aristotelian question "How should one live?" Science and literature are different tools employed by human beings to invest the world with meaning. They approach the same world, not as two cultures, but as parts of one culture, without, however, being one and the same thing. As Daniel Cordle observes, criticising a stereotypical two cultures model of science and literature does not imply "that by exposing [...] deficiencies in an established way of thinking about literature and science, one has somehow bridged the chasm and proven the equivalence of the two."[256]

4.3 Metaphysician Meets Ironist: Rationalism, Scientism, and Mysticism

In *Black Dogs* and *Enduring Love* McEwan draws upon another epistemological framework, another monumental story of the *self* which has been frequently placed in opposition to science in the history of Western culture: religion. June in *Black Dogs*, though not following the precepts of any special religion, is a mystic and metaphysician whose quest in life is the search for ultimate meaning and essential Truth. Her husband Bernard, hobby entomologist, biographer of Nasser, and Labour MP, is an atheist and rationalist, firmly rooted in the present, busy finding practical solutions to immediate problems. Jed Parry in *Enduring Love* is another mystic aspiring to a Truth beyond human understanding, and Joe, as we have seen in the preceding chapter, supports a radical scientism, rationalism, and objectivism based on material data only. The religion – science debate in *Black Dogs* and *Enduring Love* opens up a vista of questions intersecting with central questions in the literature - science debate: Are religious and scientific world-views mutually exclusive or complementary? What is the nature and purpose of human life and the universe? How is the good life lived? Yet again, McEwan makes his characters spokesmen for diverging concepts of the *self* and stories of the universe, refraining, however, from installing an authoritative voice that neatly resolves the conflict by overtly taking sides or setting up a new master narrative.

Within the framework of the marriage dispute between June and Bernard Tremaine, *Black Dogs* is organised around "two of the central themes of Western civilization: the claims of metaphysical, religious belief and materialist rationality."[257] At one point in the novel, Jeremy sums up the conflict that drove his parents-in-law apart:

---

[256] Cordle, *Postures* 41.
[257] Malcolm, *Understanding* 150.

> Rationalist and mystic, commissar and yogi, joiner and abstainer, scientist and intuitionist, Bernard and June are extremities along whose slippery axis my own disbelief slithers and never comes to rest. (*BD* 19)

Unable to subscribe to June's essentialist, metaphysical version of the world ("I felt stifled by her expressions of faith, and bothered by the unstated assumption of all believers that they are good because the believe what they believe [...]", *BD* 20) and unwilling to adopt Bernard's radical scepticism ("it was too arrogant, too much was closed off, too much denied", *BD* 19), Jeremy is caught up in a paradigmatic postmodern predicament. He is "[l]eft in the vacuum between the Scylla of epistemological and epistemic loss and the Charybdis of the impossibility of reconstructing a new master narrative."[258] As Jeremy himself puts it:

> To believe in everything, to make no choices, amounts to much the same thing, to my mind, as believing in nothing at all. I am uncertain whether our civilisation at this turn of the millennium is cursed by too much or too little belief. (*BD* 20)

In fact, the "memoir" (*BD* 19), originally planned as an attempt to reconstruct the story of June and Bernard's unhappy marriage, turns out to be to a considerable degree a "divagation" (*BD* 37) on Jeremy's part, a personal quest for a consistent framework of belief that avoids both June's essentialist metaphysics and Bernard's radical scepticism.[259]

Central to June's metaphysical world-view, is her encounter with the two black dogs of the novel's title: "As far as June was concerned, it [the encounter] was to be the centrepiece of my [Jeremy's] memoir, just as it was in her own story of her life – the defining moment, the experience that redirected, the revealed truth by whose light all previous conclusions must be re-thought" (*BD* 50). Hiking in southern France, June is attacked by two fierce, donkey-sized dogs. Miraculously she manages to fend them off with a penknife. As the beasts close in, June experiences a vision of the divine, an epiphany, or moment of Truth and godly Presence that leads her to abandon the left-wing politics she has hitherto shared with Bernard and to become a mystic recluse, refraining for the rest of her life from taking a stand in public life (*BD* 150). June's universe is "a universe filled with meaning" (*BD* 61) with no room for coincidence or contingency. She is not prepared to regard her encounter with the dogs as a chance meeting with dangerous animals run wild, but insists that the killer dogs "emanated meaning", that they embodied "[a] malign principle, a force in

---

[258] Heinz Antor, "Unreliable Narration and (Dis-)Orientation in the Postmodern Neo-Gothic Novel: Reflections on Patrick McGrath's *The Grotesque* (1989)," *Erzählen und Erzähltheorie im 20. Jahrhundert*, Anglistische Forschungen Bd. 294, ed. Jörg Helbig (Heidelberg: C. Winter, 2001) 377.
[259] Cf. Pedot, "Narration" 68.

human affairs that periodically advances to dominate and destroy lives of individuals or nations, then retreats to await the next occasion" (*BD* 19). Recounting her experience to Jeremy, June concludes:

> I met evil and I discovered God. [...] I suppose all great world religions began with individuals making inspired contact with a *spiritual reality* and then trying to keep that *knowledge* alive. [...] In the end though it hardly matters how you describe it once the *essential truth* has been grasped – that we have within us an infinite resource, a potential for a *higher state of being*, a goodness... [...] Call it God, or the spirit of love, or the Atman or the Christ or the laws of nature. [...] What matters is to make the connection with this centre, this *inner being* [emphases mine]. (*BD* 60)

June's choice of vocabulary in the passage quoted above identifies her as a staunch metaphysician who believes "that there are, out there in the world, real essences which it is our duty to discover and which are disposed to assist in their own discovery."[260] She is a believer in a true, essential *self*, firmly convinced that "human beings are something more than centreless webs of beliefs and desires."[261]

June's metaphysical concept of the *self* is based on a curious mixture of largely unspecified religious convictions, mythology, psychology, Platonism, and Enlightenment philosophy.[262] On the one hand, in keeping with the basic idea of Platonism and Christianity, June's notion of the *self* is characterised, by the "simple and uncomplicated hope to be reunited with something larger and better" than herself by "seeing through veils of illusion [...]."[263] Her faith in the existence of a True *Self* and a True Eternal Reality is grounded in her divinely "inspired contact with spiritual reality" (*BD* 60) and her insight into the human "potential for a higher state of being" (*BD* 60). As Rorty puts it, the Platonic-Christian model of the world "culminates in the ascent to the highest level of Plato's 'divided line', or the Christian Beatific Vision, or generally, in a sense of one's own identity with the larger and better being one has, unwittingly, been all the time."[264]

On the other hand, June's concept of the *self* owes much to the Enlightenment notion of the True Inner *Self* with its undividable, quasi-divine

---

[260] Rorty, *Contingency* 75.
[261] Rorty, *Contingency* 88.
[262] The books June has written and read are characteristic of the amalgam of mystical explanatory patterns in her life: *Mystical Grace: Selected Writings of St Teresa of Avila* (*BD* 172), *Ten Meditations* (*BD* 172), and Lao Tzu's *The Way of Tao* (*BD* 35). Jeremy furnishes us with a list of June's changing metaphysical convictions: "unicorns, wood spirits, angels, mediums, self-healing, the collective unconscious, the 'Christ within us'" (*BD* 46).
[263] Rorty, *Objectivity* 117.
[264] Rorty, *Objectivity* 117.

centre.[265] She variously refers to this "core of selfhood" (*BD* 60) as her "inner being" (*BD* 60), the "Christ within us" (*BD* 46), and "a luminous [...] spirit, benign and all powerful, residing within and accessible to us all" (*BD* 19). In contrast to Enlightenment philosophers like Kant, Locke, or Hume, however, June does not try to rationally determine, explain, or justify her metaphysical convictions. Rather, she contents herself with affirming and re-affirming what she believes to be the essential truth inherent in her story by building her whole life around it (*BD* 60). As Bernard tells Jeremy:

> My wife might have been interested in poetic truth, or spiritual truth, or her own private truth, but she didn't give a damn for *truth*, for the facts, for the kind of truth that two people could recognise independently of each other. She made patterns, she invented myths. Then she made the facts fit them. (*BD* 86)

Throughout her life and despite "the lengthening role call" (*BD* 46) of her changing affiliations, June never gives up on the simple, consoling dogma "that life really does have rewards and punishments, that underneath it all there's a deeper pattern of meaning beyond what we give it ourselves" (*BD* 80).

In contrast to June, Bernard is convinced that there is "no direction, no patterning in human affairs or fates other than that which [is] imposed by human minds" (*BD* 20). He likes to present himself as a specimen of what Rorty calls the ironist intellectual, i.e. a sort of person

> who faces up to the contingency of his [...] most central beliefs and desires – someone sufficiently historicist and nominalist to have abandoned the idea that those central beliefs and desires refer back to something beyond the reach of time and chance.[266]

At several points in the novel, Bernard dismisses June's metaphysical convictions as "[r]eligious cant" (*BD* 104) and "consoling magic" (*BD* 80). Rather than turn to some private mysticism like June, Bernard, throughout his life, remains loyal to the public world of first Communist and then Labour Party politics, defending his convictions with clear-cut, logical arguments (*BD* 72). A pragmatist and rationalist by nature, Bernard does not believe in unspecified "malign principles" or "perverted spirits no amount of social theory [can] account for" (*BD* 172), but regards evil as a result of wrongly implemented social and political policies, convinced that it can be corrected or eradicated by a different, rational application of the same social and political means (*BD* 73).

Submitting Bernard's rational, sceptical, pragmatist world-view to closer analysis, however, we find that it is no less categorical than June's incontrovertible belief in a meaningful universe. Bernard does not believe in a

---

[265] Cf. MacIntyre, *After Virtue* 58.
[266] Rorty, *Contingency* xv.

higher state of being or in a superhuman spiritual reality, but he is firmly, almost arrogantly, convinced of the accuracy, soundness, and superiority of his rational outlook on the world. Thus, Jeremy says about his father-in-law: "He had a way of presenting all his opinions as well-established facts, and his certainties did have a sinuous power" (*BD* 72). Confident that a "fair bout of adversarial discussion [...] bring[s] us to the truth" (*BD* 72), Bernard reduces the challenge presented to us by postmodern plurality to a simplistic dichotomy of right versus wrong. Bernard's certainty that a consensus about what is true or right or adequate in European politics can be reached through adversarial discussion is not only naïvely idealistic, but also strikingly opposed to his professed scepticism and radical denial of master narratives. Bernard might claim that "[y]ou should always keep an open mind" (*BD* 117) and stay inside what we called an ongoing discourse of values, but in fact, his rational, scientific outlook on the world is no less teleological and narrow-minded than his wife's patchwork mysticism. Reminiscing about his early communist affiliations, Bernard admits:

> It wasn't injustice that bothered me as much as untidiness. It wasn't the brotherhood of man that appealed to me so much as the efficient organisation of man. What I wanted was a society as neat as barracks, justified by scientific theories. (*BD* 77)

Bernard's obsession with scientific rationalism, tidiness, neatness, and efficiency may be more widely accepted in modern Western societies than June's vague and irrational religious convictions. This does not, however, alter the fact that Bernard's outlook on the world is, like his wife's, at heart metaphysical. Bernard's master narrative is the master narrative of science and rationalism, June's the belief in a higher spiritual reality; both partners believe in the ultimate power of their respective epistemologies to discover something more than personal truth; both are absolutists, finally unwilling to face up to the contingency of their most central beliefs and desires. Jeremy has a point when he tells Bernard: "You accused each other of the same thing. She was no more a hardliner than you are" (*BD* 90).

In *Black Dogs*, the dispute between "rational thought and spiritual insight" (*BD* 20) remains unresolved. The element of ambiguity centres on the eponymous dogs whose significance is offered up to Bernard's rational interpretation and June's mystical one. What were the black dogs? Fiends from hell? An incarnation of evil, "a viciousness against life" (*BD* 172) that "lives in us all" (*BD* 172)? An evil principle that takes hold in an individual (*BD* 172)? Or are the dogs, as Bernard believes, a literary borrowing from Churchill and Samuel Johnson (*BD* 104) and the encounter with them interpreted by June so as to allow her to take a direction in life she had already decided upon?[267] Taking the questioning even further: Did the dogs exist at all, or were they figments of June's imagination? Towards the end of the novel, the mystery of the black dogs is finally unravelled. The dogs *did* exist. As Jeremy tells us, they were guard dogs of the Gestapo abandoned during the Allied Invasion in 1944, rumoured by the population of the village St. Maurice to have been trained by the Germans to rape women (*BD* 160-162).

Still, the rational explanation of the presence of the savage animals on the country path is by no means as unambiguous and straightforward as it appears at first sight. As Malcolm points out, all the sentences that suggest that the dogs raped a woman in the village in 1944 are incomplete and the reader is required to supply the ending based on an interpretation of the context.[268] Thus, "[o]ne of the key revelations of the text turns out to be based not just on a fallible account (which it is), but on the reader's own process of interpretation."[269] We may argue that the rational explanation of the Gestapo dogs running wild is more probable than June's mystical version of her encounter with them. At the end of the novel, however, Jeremy returns to his mother-in-law's "irrational" interpretation of the dogs as embodiments of human evil, thinking of them "not as animals, but as spirit hounds, incarnations" (*BD* 173). He sees them, as June did, disappearing into the grey of dawn, moving "into the foothills of the mountains from where they will return to haunt us, somewhere in Europe, in another time" (*BD* 174).

Malcolm states that at the end of *Black Dogs*, "one has an uneasy sense that the novel as a whole might not cohere, however fascinating and brilliant it might be in its separate parts."[270] The conflict between rationality and irrationality, centring on the divergent interpretations of the black dogs, is not resolved in any final way. One can argue, however, that the novel achieves an overall coherence of design by suggesting that both rationality and irrationality are open to criticism and that both, if practised blindly, can lead to violence and the breakdown of civilised norms. In fact, "evil" and violence are frequently thematised in the novel and their sources are diverse: The father who brutally hits his son in the restaurant and the neo-Fascist skinheads with their "loose wet

---

[267] Churchill used the term 'black dog' to refer to the depression that temporarily got hold of him. Bernard suggests that June pluralised Churchill's expression to represent "a kind of cultural depression, civilisation's worst moods" (*BD* 104).

[268] Mme Auriac, proprietress of the small hotel where June and Bernard dine after June's encounter with the black dogs, tells the young couple: "I was horrified by the events of April 1944. It was a matter of deep regret…" (*BD* 160). A few lines down she states: "It wasn't the Gestapo who raped her. They used…", and finally: "The simple truth is, an animal can be trained…" (*BD* 161).

[269] Malcolm, *Understanding* 148.

[270] Malcolm, *Understanding* 153.

mouths" (*BD* 96) who attack Bernard in Berlin are animal-like in their appearance and driven by *irrational* anger, whereas the Nazi killings in the concentration camp of Majdanek (*BD* 108-110) and the "licensed violence" (*BD* 107) practised by the Communist regime in Poland are soberly executed crimes, committed in the name of perverted order and *rationality*.[271] In the end, it is up to the reader to decide where to place himself in the debate between mysticism and rationalism, metaphysics and irony. As Pedot reminds us: "L'écriture n'est pas un savoir, le savoir d'un sujet en pleine possession de son objet, mais une quête, une expérience."[272] Where this quest or experience leads us, however, depends to a large degree on our individual frameworks of belief and our previous (reading) experiences.

In *Enduring Love*, the conflict between mysticism and rationalism is removed from the domain of politics and history which shaped much of the characters' lives in *Black Dogs*, to the private domain of intimate relationships.[273] *Enduring Love* is an "epistemological thriller"[274] presenting and contrasting different kinds of knowledge, stressing at the same time the limits of describing and knowing the world through these epistemologies. As discussed in chapter 4.2, Joe Rose is an avid defender of knowledge based on facts, empirical science, traditional logic, and reason. His world-view is characterised by a firm belief in the authority of science and the sufficiency of the material world. Joe's ironist perspective leaves no room for religious interpretations or ontological accounts of morality. A modern naturalist, Joe is convinced that moral reactions are nothing but instincts or gut reactions of "obvious evolutionary utility."[275] Thus, Joe interprets the failed attempt to rescue the boy from the balloon and to avoid John Logan's death as a battle between the incommensurable instincts of altruism and selfishness "written in our nature" (*EL* 14). In an interview Ian McEwan states that he created Joe's character to depict

> a Darwinian way of looking on the world. That is, to talk about who lets go first as something that involves [...] instinct, involves an adaptationalist account of why we are what we are, quite distinct from the deist account that Jed is going to take.[276]

---

[271] The concentration camp in Majdanek is characterised by "obsessive neatness" (*BD* 110) with its huts arranged in orderly, numbered rows. Thus, despite its monstrous purpose, the 'well made' camp conveys the outward impression of a civilised settlement.
[272] Pedot, "Narration" 74.
[273] Malcolm observes that *Enduring Love* "is a return to the eerily isolated worlds of *The Cement Garden* and *The Comfort of Strangers* and a departure from the historically and socially focused worlds of *The Child in Time*, *The Innocent*, and *Black Dogs*" (Malcolm, *Understanding* 172).
[274] Malcolm, *Understanding* 157.
[275] Taylor, *Sources* 6.
[276] Reynolds and Noakes, *Ian McEwan* 16.

Joe's de-divinisation and de-mystification of the *self* and the world contrasts with both Clarissa's and Jed's teleological interpretations of the world. Clarissa believes that there is more to human life than genetically prescribed limitations and capacities (*EL* 70) and that there is a deeper purpose or meaning to the seemingly erratic, contingent forces of the universe. So, for example, she gets exasperated with Joe when he tries to analyse babies' smiles in neo-Darwinian, evolutionary terms. She claims that in Joe's theory "[e]verything was being stripped down [...] and in the process some larger meaning was lost" (*EL* 70). Similarly, discussing Logan's death with Joe, Clarissa insists that his death "must mean something" (*EL* 32). Joe coolly observes: "Logan's death was pointless – that was part of the reason we were in shock. Good people sometimes suffered and died, not because their goodness was being tested, but precisely because there was nothing, no one to test it" (*EL* 32).

Jed Parry puts forward a way of knowing the world that radically differs from Joe's. Like June in *Black Dogs*, his religious belief is vague but powerful and no amount of proof to the contrary can shatter his conviction that Joe loves him. There is no place for contingency in Parry's outlook on the world; everything has a deeper meaning and follows a divinely ordained pattern. Material facts are nothing to Parry. Joe's rationalism, scientism, and materialism are the bars of his "little cage of reason" (*EL* 133) from which Parry hopes to set his beloved free. He is firmly convinced that he can deliver Joe from meaninglessness (*EL* 136) and even when he is admitted to a mental asylum after having kidnapped Clarissa, he is able to write to Joe - whom he is forbidden to ever see again: "I feel more purpose than I've ever known in my life. I've never felt so free. I'm soaring, I'm so happy, Joe!" (*EL* 245). Immune to external proofs, Parry's capacity for self-delusion is enormous. Where Joe firmly relies on data provided by the material world, Parry completely excludes such data from his life. Or rather, Parry takes in the material world and bends it to fit his spiritual explanatory pattern. When the two men meet in front of Joe's house, for example, and Joe accidentally touches the wet leaves of a hedge in passing, Parry is convinced that Joe

> touched them in a certain way, in a pattern that spelled a simple message [...]. What a fabulous way to hear of love, through rain and leaves and skin, the pattern woven through the skein of God's sensuous creation unfolding in a scorching sense of touch. (*EL* 96)

However, although Joe's and Jed's perspectives on the world are diametrically opposed, the two men share an important trait of character. Thus, both Joe and Parry are defenders of master narratives which give their believers a considerable confidence in the truthfulness of their judgements: Joe's language is shot through with the authority of science and Jed's with the authority of religious faith. In fact, like Bernard Tremaine in *Black Dogs*, Joe Rose is no fully-fledged ironist, but a disguised metaphysician who sets up science as a master narrative, arrogantly defending it against all attacks levelled at it from the epistemological realms of literature and religion, convinced that science alone can furnish well-founded answers to the problems encountered in life. Like Bernard and June in *Black Dogs*, Joe and Jed accuse each other of the same faults. Jed writes to his beloved: "You want the final word on everything. After reading thirty-five of your articles, I should know. There is never a moment's doubt or hesitation or admission of ignorance" (*EL* 137). Similarly, Joe says about Jed: "Nothing could prove him wrong, nothing needed to prove him right. If I had written a letter declaring passionate love, it would have made no difference. He crouched in a cell of his own devising" (*EL* 143). Interestingly, Joe's reference to Parry crouching in a cell of his own devising mirrors Jed's statement about Joe being trapped in his "little cage of reason" (*EL* 133) quoted above. The image of the cage or cell is taken up again by Joe when Clarissa leaves him alone in their flat and paranoid feelings begin to flood over him. Joe tells us: "I felt like a mental patient at the end of visiting hours. *Don't leave me here with my mind*, I thought. *Get them to let me out*" (*EL* 58).

However, the mental patient in *Enduring Love* is Jed Parry; it is the religious bigot and not the rational scientist who is transferred to the closed ward of a mental asylum. Joe, as we have seen in the preceding chapter, is right both about Parry's illness and the danger he constitutes in his delusional state. Looking back on the novel as a whole, we find that knowledge about the world is presented as uncertain, difficult to achieve, open to constant revision, but that it is still attainable in some way. All forms of knowledge are not equal in *Enduring Love*. In fact, there are "better" and "worse" ways of approaching reality, even in our postmodern age where the awareness of relativity and contingency might tempt us to subscribe to an outlook on the world in which "anything goes". Joe's rationalism, scientism, and materialism does not make him popular with his girlfriend, but it *does* save her from being killed by a madman. For all the reservations we may have about Joe's vision of the world, his emotional blandness and arrogance, his version of events turns out to be closer to reality than that of either Clarissa or the police. As Malcolm concludes: "Joe may be frustrating to Clarissa, but – barring the possibility that the whole novel is meant to be read as an extensive piece of lying – his stubborn rationality is the best bet in the chaos of human impulses."[277]

---

[277] Malcolm, *Understanding* 179.

5. At the Crossroads: The Impact of the Singular on the Concept of the *Self*

5.1 Dealing with Epistemological Crises: Redescriptions and New Horizons

In chapter four we analysed *The Child in Time, Black Dogs, Enduring Love*, and *Atonement* with reference to the explanatory patterns, paradigms of knowledge or stories of the *self* provided by literature, science, and religion. We found that even though the characters' perspectives on the world differ - ranging from the denial of intrinsic structures of meaning to the unquestioned affirmation of the fundamental meaningfulness of the universe - McEwan's protagonists equal one another in their efforts to structure the world according to some explanatory pattern which for them is ranked incomparably higher than all other explanatory patterns on offer. Even sceptics like Bernard and Joe hold fast to the notion of the ultimate explicability of the world and are loath to step outside their clearly demarcated rationalist framework of belief. As McEwan aptly observes, believing in something is "an enduring quality of being human – perhaps even written into our natures. No amount of science or logic will shift it. We are all magical thinkers one way or another."[278]

As we have seen in our discussion of identity and orientation in chapter three, believing in something, taking an individual standpoint, a perspective, in moral space, is inextricably linked to our sense of undamaged, consistent selfhood. In fact, Taylor points out,

> [t]o know who you are is to be oriented in moral space, a space in which questions arise about what is good or bad, what is worth doing and what not, what has a meaning and importance to you and what is trivial and secondary.[279]

We turn to stories of the *self* and the world provided by science, religion, mythology, literature, or philosophy to answer these questions, to find framework-definitions that provide the horizon within which we know where we stand and what meaning things have for us.[280] Having attained a basic sense of orientation in moral space, we are capable of accounting for our*selves* in the various contexts of moral life, able to determine from case to case what is good or bad, valuable or worthless, what we ought to affirm or oppose.

---

[278] *Bold Type*, "An Interview with Ian McEwan," *Bold Type 2.9* (1998), 10 Dec. 2002 <http://www.randomhouse.com/ boldtype/0398/mcewan/interview.html>.
[279] Taylor, *Sources* 28.
[280] Taylor, *Sources* 29.

Does this imply that all we have to do in life is find a suitable framework of belief, stick to it and be henceforth able to safely and infallibly judge ourselves, other people, and the situations we encounter? Does clinging single-mindedly to an explanatory pattern permanently secure us against the frightening experience of being lost in a void of contingency? In pre-modern times, when the good life was still incontestably and universally ordained by religious tenets which claimed "institutional hegemony",[281] and "people saw their frameworks as enjoying the same ontological solidity as the very structure of the universe",[282] the above might have applied. Today, however, where we are exposed to a great number of explanatory patterns with no clearly demarcated hierarchical structure, frameworks once solid and unassailable have become permeable. Meaning no longer resides in a single, unchallengeable master narrative and our individual horizons remain open to constant redescription.

In the four novels discussed in this paper, Ian McEwan reminds us of the precariousness, complexity, and difficulty of modern (value) commitments by putting his characters' explanatory patterns to the test in situations that exceed the ordinary or familiar. Contingency enters the protagonists' lives in the form of singular, unprecedented events that shatter the horizon of expectation and forseeability. Realising that the frameworks of belief which successfully worked for them so far do not furnish them with effective methods of coping with the contingency that has taken hold of their lives, the protagonists of McEwan's novels lose their formerly secure footing in moral space. Having stepped outside the horizon within which some possibilities appear to take on more significance than others, the meaning of such possibilities becomes "unfixed, labile, or undetermined."[283] As a result, McEwan's characters suffer an epistemological crisis, feeling a kind of vertigo before the questions "Who am I?" and "How is the good life lived?"[284] Taylor describes the failure to answer these questions as an experience of unbearable lack, "an acute form of disorientation",[285] a terrifying emptiness which is diametrically opposed to the sense of fullness and wholeness of the *self* after which human beings strive in their lives.

The existential yearning for wholeness and consistency, for a world that is ultimately explicable in terms of a coherent framework of belief, induces the characters to search for new structures of meaning that help them grasp the singular, unclassified, idiosyncratic, to conceptualise and thus incorporate it into the realm of the familiar. As Antor elucidates:

---

[281] MacIntyre, *After Virtue* 173.
[282] Taylor, *Sources* 26.
[283] Taylor, *Sources* 28.
[284] Nicholas H. Smith, "Contingency and Self-Identity: Taylor's Hermeneutics vs. Rorty's Postmodernism," *Theory, Culture & Society* 13.2 (1996): 108.
[285] Taylor, *Sources* 27.

> Man is a pattern-building animal, and if the traditional explanatory patterns we are confronted with do not seem adequate to what we perceive and cannot account for the phenomena we are confronted with, we either redefine them until they fit again or we replace them by others of a greater complexity which can yet again re-establish a consistent order at a higher level.[286]

To re-establish a consistent order in their lives, McEwan's protagonists universally fall back on narrative as "the preferred, perhaps even [...] obligatory medium"[287] of structuring their experience. In other words, in all four novels, the horizon-breaking breach with the ordinary triggers "the rich dynamic of narrative – how to cope with it, domesticate it, to get things back on a familiar track."[288] At the end of the process, the characters reconnect to a story of the *self* and the world that makes sense "across the whole range of both explanatory and life uses",[289] that places them yet again inside a qualitative horizon that provides a best account of the life they are currently leading.[290]

In *The Child in Time*, Kate's mysterious disappearance shakes Stephen's formerly stable marriage to the roots; he realises that Julie's and his "old intimacy, their habitual assumption that they were on the same side, was dead" (*CT* 19). The loss of his daughter breaks up Stephen's familiar assumptions about grief, love and mutual understanding: "Everything before had been fantasy, a routine and frenetic mimicry of sorrow" (*CT* 20-21). Bereft of a centre in his life that provides a fixed point of orientation, Stephen's world "loses altogether its spiritual contour."[291] He is no longer able to perform the basic pattern-building activities of naming, labelling, and categorizing that in ordinary circumstances help us ward off the frightening experience of arbitrariness: "[A]ll about him shapes without definition drifted and dissolved, lost to categories" (*CT* 10). Caught in a nameless space of contingency, Stephen does not only lose his sense of orientation and the ability to account for his actions, but he is deprived of consistent selfhood, he is "barely a conscious being at all" (*CT* 11). In the year following the disappearance of his daughter, Stephen continues to exist in a "semantic vacuum",[292] feeling "empty of time, dry of meaning or purpose" (*CT* 30). Unable to "transform the [...] chaotic contingency of the world into [...] meaningful causal consistency",[293] Stephen cannot "generate a

---

[286] Heinz Antor, "The Arts, the Sciences, and the Making of Meaning: Tom Stoppard's *Arcadia* as a Post-Structuralist Play," *Anglia* 116 (1998): 336.
[287] Bruner, *Making Stories* 89.
[288] Bruner, *Making Stories* 89.
[289] Taylor, *Sources* 58.
[290] Taylor, *Sources* 58.
[291] Taylor, *Sources* 18.
[292] Antor, "Arts and Sciences" 336.
[293] Antor, "Arts and Sciences" 336.

motive" (*CT* 38) even for simple daily procedures like washing, shaving, and, dressing himself.

After the first phase of immobilising shock and total disorientation, Stephen and Julie set out separately to re-organise their lives, searching for frameworks that can restore meaning to their existence. In her retreat at the Chilterns, Julie spends her time composing music and "reading mystical or sacred texts – St John of the Cross, Blake's longer poems, Lao-tzu" (*CT* 49); She tries to counteract contingency by turning to the structured language of poetry, the teleological pattern of religion and the abstract, formalised language of musical symbols. Julie knows that she must reassess her habitual horizon to incorporate the loss of her daughter, that she must "set about transforming herself, purposefully evolve some different understanding of life and her place within it" (*CT* 50) if she wants to regain a firm footing in moral space. Stephen compares his wife's dynamic concept of the *self* with his own, static one:

> Such faith in endless mutability, in re-making yourself as you came to understand more, or changed your version, he had come to see as an aspect of her [Julie's] femininity. [...] Past a certain age, men froze into place, they tended to believe that, even in adversity, they were somehow at one with their fates. Despite what they said, men believed in what they did and they stuck at it. (*CT* 51)

In keeping with his masculine credo, Stephen does not change or redefine his horizon to make room for the loss of his daughter, but rather avoids facing the loss altogether by giving himself the illusionary comfort that he is "the father of an invisible child" (*CT* 2). As we have already stated in 4.2, however, Thelma's quantum magic fails to work for him and Stephen finally realises that he has to come to terms with his daughter's unexplained disappearance if he ever wants to resume a life that is purposeful and fulfilling. Like Julie, Stephen now turns to structured, rule-governed activities that can provide provisional patterns of meaning and orientation instead of pointlessly running after Kate and day-dreaming about her existence in a parallel universe: "The idea was to shake himself awake by learning something difficult; he wanted rules and their exceptions and the grim absorption of learning by heart" (*CT* 156). Thus, Stephen divides his time between learning ancient Arabic (*CT* 156) and playing tennis (*CT* 157), slowly but steadily regaining a grip on his life.

When Stephen finds out towards the end of the novel that an early attempt at reconciliation has let to Julie's becoming pregnant, he claims that "all the sorrow, all the empty waiting had been enclosed within meaningful time, within the richest unfolding conceivable" (*CT* 213). Stephen's speculations about the meaningful patterning of time effect a major shift in the novel "towards ideas of providential predestination, a planned view of time, and traditional metaphysics of fate that are quite at odds with the quantum."[294] The birth of the new child closes the ontological and epistemological gap created by Kate's abduction; it makes retroactive sense of the empty time of purposeless existence and reduces the endless number of competing realities that Thelma's quantum magic promised to a single "real" world. It appears that in times of epistemological crisis the borderless, timeless universe of infinite possibilities envisaged by new science offers no effective consolation. As human beings, we need to position ourselves in *one* world, we must choose a position in moral space and not "forever remain in the space between various interpretations or evaluations."[295] Thus, shortly before the baby's birth Stephen and Julie face the finality and irreversibility of their loss together, crying for "the lost, irreplaceable child who would not grow older for them, whose characteristic look and movement could never be dispelled by time" (*CT* 217). Both partners are aware that the baby can constitute a new, meaningful centre in their lives, that "while they could never redeem the loss of their daughter, they would love her through their new child, and never close their minds to the possibility of her return" (*CT* 217).[296]

June's encounter with the *Black Dogs* during her honeymoon constitutes a horizon-breaking event in the aftermath of which her life changes fundamentally. Rambling through the wild and untamed countryside, June is frightened by the thought that the well-ordered universe, the new, post-war Europe of social justice (*BD* 138) that she and Bernard philosophised about only the day before on the Dolmen, may be nothing but a youthful, idealistic illusion. Looking down on a river etched deep into a mountain range, June observes:

> The proper response [to the countryside] was fear. She half remembered reading the accounts of eighteenth-century travellers in the Lake District and the Swiss Alps. Mountain peaks were terrifying, plummeting gorges were horrible, untamed nature was a chaos, a post-lapsarian rebuke, a dread reminder. (*BD* 142)

Like the Romantic travel writers before her, June is awed and intimidated by the impact of the sublime epitomised in the rough, chaotic nature of the mountain scenery. Facing the contingent chaos of untamed nature, June is gripped by "a sourceless fear" (*BD* 141), a "nameless anxiety" (*BD* 141), and "deep nausea" (*BD* 141) that unsettles her formerly stable *self*-definition as "a young mother-

---

[294] Wright, "Physics" 229.
[295] Antor, "Ethics" 75.
[296] Note in this context that the lost centre in Stephen and Julie's life mirrors the "loss of the centre" that characterises our (post)modern existence. Just as Kate's loss remains unredeemed in the novel, we "postmoderns" are aware of the fact that the lost centre of our metaphysical past cannot be retrieved and that all we can do in a post-teleological age is create provisional centres of meaning, none of which, however, can "lay claim to representing truth and reality as such [...] and [...] aspire to the status of ultimate authority" (Antor, "Unreliable Narration" 372).

to-be in love with her husband, a socialist and optimist, compassionately rational, free of superstitions, on a walking tour in the country [...], seizing the last days of carefree holiday before England, responsibility, winter" (*BD* 142). Later the same day, when June comes face to face with the huge dogs, her feelings of "nameless, unreasonable, unmentionable disquiet" (*BD* 145) peak. Though she is scared of the animals' presence on the country path, she is even more frightened by "the possibility of their absence, of their not existing at all" (*BD* 145). Thus, what June is afraid of most is a semantic vacuum, a "chasm of meaninglessness" (*BD* 49) in which all frameworks of belief that promised to provide a meaningful interpretation of the *self* and the universe evaporate into nothingness.

June reacts to the intimidating experience of absence by replacing her rationalist explanatory pattern with a mystical one, hoping it will secure her against the epistemological void experienced on her walk through the "gothic" countryside: "She tried to find the space within her for the presence of God and thought she discerned the faintest outlines, a significant emptiness she had never noticed before, at the back of her skull" (*BD* 149). The encounter with the black dogs constitutes a turning point or "self-generated peripeteia"[297] in the history of June's *self*-telling; it structures her life (before and after the revelation), fills it with meaning, and legitimises the changes in her life that followed the encounter ("Why she left the party, why she and Bernard fell into a lifetime's disharmony, why she reconsidered her rationalism, [...] how she came to live the life she did, where she lived it, what she thought", *BD* 50). When Jeremy visits June in an old peoples' home in Wiltshire in 1987, he criticises his mother-in-law for trying to bridge the "void" (*BD* 50) and alleviate the "vertigo" (*BD* 50) of meaninglessness by making the black dogs the focal- or turning point of her life that "explain[s] everything" (*BD* 50). Jeremy declares in an offhand way that

> [t]urning-points are the inventions of storytellers and dramatists, a necessary mechanism when a life is reduced to, traduced by, a plot, when morality must be distilled from a sequence of actions, when an audience must be sent home with something unforgettable to mark a character's growth. (*BD* 50)

As long as we remember, however, that the turning points in our lives are *self*-created and not ordained by "fate" or discovered, there is no danger in including them into our *self*-interpreting narratives. In fact, Bruner points out, "one rarely encounters autobiographies, whether spontaneously told or written in interview, that are without turning points."[298] Turning points provide landmarks of orientation in moral space; they contribute to a meaningful, coherent plot - i.e. a scheme, design, plan, or pattern in our lives that connects a sequence of events

---

[297] Bruner, *Making Stories* 83.
[298] Bruner, *Making Stories* 83.

in a way that emphasises their causality - making it possible for us to answer questions like "Why did it happen?" and "What is going to happen next?" June is aware of the meaning-giving, pattern-building function her pivotal encounter with the black dogs has in her life:

> I know that everyone thinks I've made too much of it – a young girl frightened by a couple of dogs on a country path. But you wait until you come to make sense of your life. You'll either find you're too old and lazy to make the attempt, or you'll do what I have done, single out a certain event, find in something ordinary and explicable a means of expressing what might otherwise be lost to you. [...] I'm not saying that these animals were anything other than what they appeared to be [...]. I don't actually believe they were Satan's familiars, Hell Hounds, or omens from God. [...] I haven't mythologised these animals. I've made use of them. (*BD* 59)

In contrast to June, Joe in *Enduring Love* is proud of staring the beast of contingency unflinchingly in the eye. He mocks the attempts of his girlfriend to search for a deeper meaning and a larger purpose in life and coolly remarks that everything can be reduced to the "earthbound scale of the biological" (*EL* 207). However, as we have already observed before, Joe's ironist scepticism and scientific certitude is shaken in the course of the novel. The ballooning accident and the chain of consequences that succeed it, put Joe's rationalism to the test, subtly but irrevocably widening his horizon and changing his *self*-definition as a sober scientist. Joe himself describes the ballooning accident as "a catastrophe, which [...] was a kind of furnace in whose heat identities and fates would buckle into new shapes" (*EL* 3). Although Joe's interpretation of Parry's madness turns out to be right, there are moments in the novel when he comes close to exchanging his Darwinian outlook on the world for a reassuring metaphysical one. When Joe watches John Logan fall, for instance, he clings to the irrational hope that "some beam, or god, or some other impossible cartoon thing came and gathered him up" (*EL* 16), hoping that the law of "ruthless gravity" (*EL* 16) can temporarily be revoked.[299]

Joe spends the day following the accident in the London Library, experiencing feelings of apprehension he can neither explain nor control. He is firmly convinced that Parry is following him, but as there is no proof of this as yet, Joe's anxiety remains threateningly vague. Thus, he tells us: "I was afraid of my fear, because I did not yet know the cause. I was scared of what it would do to me and what it would make me do" (*EL* 44). A few pages later Joe says about

---

[299] Similarly, when Joe first realises that he might be the victim of a stalker, he tries to counteract his fear by performing a superstitious gesture. He straightens up an overturned jam jar of flowers placed on the pavement where a policewoman has been shot. Joe states: "I couldn't help feeling as I pushed the jar closer to the railings[...] that it might bring luck, or rather protection, and that on such hopeful acts of propitiation [...] whole religions where founded [...]" (*EL* 44-45).

Parry: "[H]e represented the unknown, into which I projected all kinds of inarticulate terrors" (*EL* 69). The nameless, unpredictable, and uncategorised frightens Joe as it directly and personally confronts him with the contingency and arbitrariness of the universe which he has hitherto only theoretically and detachedly discussed in his scientific articles. Brought face to face with arbitrariness in "real" life, i.e. meeting contingency incarnate in the form of Jed Parry, Joe realises that neither rationalism nor logic can insulate him from the frightening experience of being exposed to erratic, uncontrollable forces. He has to admit that Parry is "inviolable in his solipsism" and that "[t]he logic that might drive him from despair to hatred, or from love to destruction in one leap, [is] private, unguessable" (*EL* 144).

The experience of being exposed to the unforeseeable and uncontrollable, triggers off a pattern-building process in the course of which Joe tries to domesticate the unfamiliar by integrating it into the realm of the known and predictable. Thus, when Joe is finally able to put a name-tag to Parry's madness, his life regains structure, purpose, and orientation:

> De Clérambault's syndrome. The name was like a fanfare, a clear trumpet sound recalling me to my own obsessions. There was research to follow through now and I knew exactly where to start. A syndrome was *a framework of prediction* [emphasis mine] and it offered a kind of comfort. (*EL* 124)

However, placing Parry's disorder within the borders of de Clérambault's syndrome does not render his actions more predictable. In fact, all that Joe's research on Parry's condition amounts to is a renewed confirmation of the latter's unpredictability (*EL* 143). Hence, when Parry takes Clarissa hostage it comes as a real shock to Joe (*EL* 204). In an effort to counteract his increasing fear of the unforeseeable outcome of the hostage-taking he turns to the down-to-earth, predictable narrative of evolutionary biology:

> What I thought might calm me was the reminder that, for all our concerns, we were still part of [a] natural dependency – for the animals that we ate grazed the plants which, like our vegetables and fruits, were nourished by the soil that formed these organisms. (*EL* 207)

In the context of his acute anxiety about Clarissa, however, the clearly structured pattern of the all-encompassing cycle of life offers neither consolation nor practical help. Hence, Joe states:

> I could not believe in the primary significance of these grand cycles. Just beyond the oxygen-exhaling trees stood my poison-exuding vehicle, inside which was my gun, and thirty-five miles down teeming roads was the enormous city on whose northern side was my apartment where a madman was waiting, a de Clérambault, my de Clérambault, and my threatened loved one. What, in this description, was necessary to

the carbon cycle, or the fixing of nitrogen? *We were no longer in the great chain. It was our own complexity that had expelled us from the Garden* [emphasis mine]. (*EL* 207)

In this passage, Joe denies the explanatory superiority of the abstract language of modern science and turns instead to the epistemologies of metaphysics and theology ("the great chain [of being]", "the Garden [of Eden]"). The internal contradiction apparent in the mixing up of the vocabulary of evolutionary biology and chemistry with a religious vocabulary constitutes the climax of a series of inconsistencies that impair Joe's *self*-image as a pure-blood scientist.[300] At the end of *Enduring Love*, Joe is no longer the arrogant defender of a rationalist scientific master narrative whom we got to know on the preceding 200 or so pages. Joe's horizon has changed in the course of events; he is now even able to state, when Clarissa is finally released and Parry hospitalised with a bullet wound from Joe's gun, that "there isn't only ever one system of logic" (*EL* 214). When Joe and Clarissa meet again on an outing with Logan's widow and her children ten days after the shooting, Joe wonders whether he and Clarissa will eventually forgive each other and rekindle their relationship. Strikingly, for the first time in the novel Joe admits: "I just did not know" (*EL* 230).

In *Atonement*, thirteen-year-old Briony Tallis is a stranger to these words. When she accuses Robbie Turner of her cousin Lola's rape, she is firmly convinced that he has committed the crime: "She had no doubt. She could describe him. There was nothing she could not describe" (*A* 165). A few pages later Briony states: "If her poor cousin was not able to command the truth, then she would do it for her. *I can. And I will*" (*A* 168). Only in her late teens, when "ruthless youthful forgetting [and] wilful erasing" (*A* 171) have given way to a painful awareness of her guilt, does she grasp the full significance of her false accusation. Briony spends the rest of her long life trying to atone for a testimony the consequences of which she could or would not foresee at the time of "her crime" (*A* 156).

Seventeen-year-old Briony chastises herself for her wrongdoing by denying herself a university education at Girton college and by taking up wartime nursing in a London hospital instead. However, Briony's drudgery at the hospital under the strict rule of Sister Drummond does not reconcile her to her guilt, but rather numbs her feelings and alienates her from any sense of autonomy and consistent selfhood:

> Briony thought that she was joining the war effort. In fact, she had narrowed her life to a relationship with a woman fifteen years older who assumed a power over her greater

---

[300] See pages 57-58 and 77-78 of this paper.

than that of a mother over an infant. This narrowing [...] was above all *a stripping away of identity* [emphasis mine]. (*A* 275)

Briony, now Nurse Tallis with "no identity beyond her badge" (*A* 276), abandons herself to an "unthinking obedience" (*A* 275) that closes down her "mental horizons" (*A* 275). The daily routine at the hospital vacates her mind (*A* 276) and reduces her life to a simple pattern of "strictures, rules, obedience, housework, and a constant fear of disapproval" (*A* 276).

Still, Briony's *self*-denial as "a maid, a skivvy and [...] a crammer of simple facts" (*A* 277) does not insulate her permanently from the feeling of guilt and from the nascent "unease that was out there in the streets as well as in the wards, and was like darkness itself. Nothing in her routine, not even Sister Drummond, could protect her from it" (*A* 277). The unease Briony experiences in 1940 is indicative of a change that is taking place in Briony's private life as well as all over Europe. Briony's growing awareness of her wrongdoing, of the chaos and upheaval she caused in Robbie's and Cecilia's lives, is mirrored in the chaos and the contingency of the Second World War which "usher[d] in a radically different postmodern era."[301] When Briony writes down the first, modernist version of the many drafts that recapture the events of the fatal summer's day in 1935, she tries to tame the chaos of her emotions by focussing on the story's formal structure, shirking a deeper (moral) involvement with plot and character:

> What exited her about her achievement was its design, the pure geometry and the defining uncertainty which reflected, she thought, a modern sensibility. The age of clear answers was over. So was the age of characters and plots. [...] The very concept of character was founded on errors that modern psychology had exposed. Plots too were like rusted machinery whose wheels would no longer turn. A modern novelist could no more write characters and plots than a modern composer could a Mozart symphony. (*A* 281)

The fact that "the age of clear answers is over", however, does not imply that the age of asking questions has likewise come to an end. As Taylor reminds us, questions about our identity, about where we are placed in moral space, and about where we are going "inescapably pre-exist for us, independent of our answer or inability to answer."[302] Briony finally realises that she has to face her guilt, that she cannot evade the question of her culpability by hiding "behind some borrowed notions of modern writing, and drown her guilt in a stream –

---

[301] Finney, "Briony's Stand". Robbie, whose old life is brought to a sudden, traumatic end by Briony's false accusation, reflects on the connection between his private pain and the public pain caused by the war: "A dead civilization. First his own life ruined, then everybody else's" (*A* 217).
[302] Taylor, *Sources* 30.

three streams! – of consciousness [...]" (*A* 320). When 77-year-old Briony looks back on the story of her life, the issues of guilt and atonement still preoccupy her:

> The problem in these fifty-nine years has been this: how can a novelist achieve atonement when, with her absolute power of deciding outcomes, she is also God? There is no one, no entity or higher form that she can appeal to, or be reconciled with, or that can forgive her. There is nothing outside her. In her imagination she has set the limits and the terms. No atonement for God, or novelists, even if they are atheists. It was always an impossible task, and that was precisely the point. The attempt was all. (*A* 371)

In the end, there is no atonement for Briony, as the only two people who could forgive her have long since died. Being an atheist, there is no higher entity she can appeal to, no God to absolve her of her guilt. Her questions remain unanswered. Still, Briony realises that her chance to finally find some peace of mind lies precisely in the impossibility of the task she has set herself: If there is no atonement for her, if the possibility of it has been excluded from the outset, then attempting to achieve atonement has been sufficient, has been all she could have possibly done. The story Briony comes up with in her final draft is the best account she can give, a version in which Robbie and Cecilia are reunited and some "hope [and] satisfaction" (*A* 371) is retained. Having dabbled in modernist impartiality, survived a World War, and penned half a dozen pitiless drafts in which Robbie and her sister are denied a happy reunion (*A* 370), Briony deliberately, *self*-consciously decides to let her last version end on a compassionate, benign note. She tells herself:

> I like to think that it isn't weakness or evasion, but a final act of kindness, a stand against oblivion and despair, to let my lovers live and to unite them at the end. I gave them happiness, but I was not so self-serving as to let them forgive me. (*A* 372)

Thus, Briony is only partly right when she says about her final draft that she has "made a huge digression and doubled back to [her] starting place" (*A* 370), to the play she wrote when she was thirteen. Although her "lovers end well" (*A* 370), as did the lovers in her early play, Briony has travelled and in the course of six decades her horizon has widened.

5.2 Love, Loss, and Guilt: The Emotional Geography of the *Self*

As the discussion of epistemological crises in *The Child in Time, Black Dogs, Enduring Love,* and *Atonement* has shown, the difference between coherent selfhood and fragmented selfhood, between a good life and what we would like to call "mere existence", depends on our ability to discriminate between the worthwhile and the worthless, the fulfilling and the vacuous, the meaningful and the meaningless in the changing contexts of our lives. We saw that the inability to answer the questions "Who am I?" and "Where am I going?" does not make the question go away. On the contrary, as Nicholas Smith argues, the force of an epistemological crisis "is just that the question of what is really of more or less importance, worthwhile or fulfilling, demands an answer even if we are not in a position to give one."[303] Indeed, Taylor asserts, only upon the supposition that the question of the good life arises independently of our ability to answer it, does the possibility of failing to answer it make sense.[304] Still, the fact that we are inescapably and non-contingently extended in a space of moral questions does not rule out contingency at the level of *how* we are orientated in this space. In fact, as Smith emphasises, Taylor's hermeneutics crucially presuppose "the absence of the kind of metaphysical foundation which would fully close the self off to contingency."[305] In other words, the values or hypergoods that define our qualitative horizons, that make best sense of our mental lives and help us define our identity, are contingent upon our individual cultural and social background; they are, as Taylor puts it, "contestable answers to inescapable questions."[306]

How do we arrive at individual hypergoods and best accounts in our lives? Put differently: How do we convince ourselves that a certain perspective on the world is best suited to endow our life with meaning and furnish the sense of 'at-one-ment' that characterises the good life? Taylor holds that best accounts are attained via practical reasoning, i.e. a reasoning in transitions which is "concerned covertly or openly, implicitly or explicitly, with comparative propositions."[307] If I find that the move from A to B is an error-reducing one, if I realise, for example, that a mystic outlook (B) on the world helps me explain a phenomenon encountered in the world that a scientific outlook (A) cannot account for, I regard view B as superior to view A because I have lived through a transition which I have come to understand as an epistemic gain.[308]

However, practical reasoning alone does not answer the question why people turn to one hypergood or explanatory pattern at a given point in their lives rather than to a another, equally well-suited one. Particularly, it does not account for the fervour and energy with which people sometimes defend the most erroneous or *self*-damaging convictions. In fact, Taylor admits that there is

---

[303] Smith, "Contingency and Self-Identity" 109.
[304] Taylor, *Sources* 30.
[305] Smith, "Contingency and Self-Identity" 109.
[306] Taylor, *Sources* 41.
[307] Taylor, *Sources* 72.
[308] Taylor, *Sources* 72f. Note that perspective B does not offer access to some ultimate Truth, but - as a provisional best account - remains open to challenge in future contexts of moral life.

more to the good life than reasoned transitions from one hypergood to another. He points out that

> our acceptance of any hypergood is connected in a complex way with our being *moved* by it. [...] We are moved by it seeing its point as something infinitely valuable. We experience our love for it as a well-founded love. Nothing that couldn't move me in *this* way would count as a hypergood.[309]

While Taylor, in his analysis of the modern *self*, still remains cautiously vague about the emotional aspect of value commitments, Martha Nussbaum devotes her recent study *Upheavals of Thought* entirely to a cognitive-evaluative appraisal of emotions such as grief, love, loss, guilt, or compassion. She argues that emotions are more than gut reactions, that they "involve [...] judgments in which, appraising an external object as salient for our own well-being, we acknowledge our own neediness and incompleteness before parts of the world that we do not fully control."[310] Starting with an account of the experience of grief felt at her mother's death, Nussbaum explores the *eudaimonistic* nature of emotions, i.e. their contribution to human flourishing, the good life, and "all to which the [individual moral] agent ascribes intrinsic value."[311] Emotions, Nussbaum elaborates, shape the moral topography of our lives, they enter intelligently into our perceptions and beliefs, and are ineradicably linked to what matters to us as individuals. In other words,

> [e]motions contain an ineliminable reference to *me*, to [...] *my* scheme of goals and projects. They see the world from my point of view. The fact that it is *my* mother is not simply a fact like any other fact about the world: it is what structures the geography of the whole situation, and we cannot capture the emotion without including that element. [...] In short, the evaluations associated with emotions are evaluations from *my* perspective, not from some impartial perspective; they contain an ineliminable reference to the self.[312]

Since emotions always refer to the *self*, since they are strong markers of perspective and thus incontestably part of an individual life story, we cannot sidestep them in our discussion of storytelling and the concept of the *self*. Indeed, in all four novels analysed in this paper, emotions like love, loss, fear, and guilt contribute both to the propelling of the respective plot and to the development of the protagonists' character or *ethos*. The contingency that enters the characters' lives directly touches upon what is valuable and salient in the protagonists' world, causing emotional upheavals in the grip of which the

---

[309] Taylor, *Sources* 73f.
[310] Nussbaum, *Upheavals* 19.
[311] Nussbaum, *Upheavals* 32.
[312] Nussbaum, *Upheavals* 52.

characters realise their own "passivity before the ungoverned events of life."[313] As Nussbaum explains:

> [T]he reason why in some emotional experiences the self feels torn apart (and in happier experiences filled with a marvellous sense of wholeness) is [...] that these are transactions with a world about which we care deeply, a world that may complete us or tear us apart. No view that makes the emotion just like a physical object hitting us can do justice to the way the world enters into the self in emotion, with enormous power to wound or heal. For it enters in a cognitive way, in our perceptions and beliefs about what matters.[314]

In *The Child in Time*, for example, the grief and the sense of loss caused by Kate's unexplained disappearance set a plot rolling in the course of which Stephen and Julie reweave the torn fabric of their lives and finally experience a sense of wholeness of the *self* through the love for their new child and their reawakened love for each other. In *Black Dogs*, a strong fear of meaninglessness and emptiness induces June to reconstruct her life around a Presence that can provide epistemological security. Jeremy's search for a "hearth" is, above all, a quest for the wholeness of the *self* that love can furnish, whereas in *Enduring Love*, the potentially healing power of love is turned by Jed Parry into a destructive force that dismantles Joe and Clarissa's relationship.

In *Atonement*, Briony's strong sense of guilt irreversibly shapes the landscape of her mental and social life, "[refining] the methods of self-torture, threading the beads of detail into an eternal loop, a rosary to be fingered for a lifetime" (*A* 173). As a member of the family of emotions, guilt constitutes an evaluation from Briony's personal perspective, an ineliminable reference to her*self*, making it impossible for her to remain the impartial observer of modernist writing. Guilt induces Briony to take up wartime nursing in a London hospital, to renounce a university education, to sever ties with her family, and to continually re-live the fatal day in the summer of 1935 when she blighted both Robbie's and her sister's lives by letting her novelist's imagination run riot. Why does the feeling of guilt never wane in the course of sixty years? Why is the search for atonement still the unquestioned *telos* of the ageing author's life, even as her conscious *self* is about to be undone by an Alzheimer's-like disorder characterised by a "loss of memory, short- and long-term, [...] then language itself, along with balance, and soon after, all motor control and finally the autonomous nervous system" (*A* 354-355)?

Nussbaum asserts that emotions such as grief or guilt often stay with us over long periods of time, because the experience of these emotions "contains rich and dense perceptions [...] which are highly concrete and replete with

---

[313] Nussbaum, *Upheavals* 78.
[314] Nussbaum, *Upheavals* 78.

detail."[315] Thus, Briony's enduring experience of guilt is not just due to an abstract realisation of her culpability, but involves a host of detailed memories that have a connection "to the concrete picturing of events in [her] imagination."[316] In other words, Briony would not continue to feel guilty if she was unable to picture the summer's day of 60 years ago vividly in her imagination; she would not go on caring for Robbie and Cecilia as part of her "scheme of goals and projects" if she was unable to richly and compassionately imagine the lovers' pain, anger, and distress caused by her false accusation.

The vivid imagination that allows 77-year-old Briony to project herself into the feelings and thoughts of Robbie and her sister, that enables her to grant them an existence outside her own experience, to conjure up what it must have felt like for Robbie to take part in the retreat from Dunkirk and for Cecilia to be forcibly separated from her lover and estranged from her family, is strikingly different from the kind of imagination that caused her to write Robbie into her story as a "villain" in 1935. Briony's youthful imagination ruthlessly and egoistically subordinated the world and other people to schemes and patterns gleaned from an uncritical reading of telic narratives such as fairy-tales; it forced life to conform to an aesthetic orderliness that completely ignored the voices of the other and strove to eliminate "the confusion of feeling contradictory things" (*A* 116).

The novel that we read, and that took Briony all her adult life to write, is an attempt at atoning for the myopic, *self*-centred imagination that destroyed Robbie's and Cecilia's lives. Briony's refusal at the end of the novel - and, in fact, at the end of her life - to have the lovers forgive her even in her fictional account of their happy survival (*A* 371), furnishes a final proof that in her quest for atonement Briony has learned how to imaginatively put herself into the position of other people. By denying herself forgiveness - and hence the possibility of achieving atonement - Briony abandons her role as an autonomous Author-God who is wholly separate, aloof, and in full control of her creation.[317]

---

[315] Nussbaum, *Upheavals* 65.

[316] Nussbaum, *Upheavals* 65.

[317] Moreover, Briony's acknowledgement of the impossibility of achieving atonement by writing down a final version of her "crime" marks her as a truly postmodern writer. Unlike Proust's narrator, Marcel, in *A la recherche du temps perdu* (1913-1927), for example, whose search for the past proclaimed by the novel's title is vindicated by the discovery that the past - in its true version - is eternally alive in the unconscious and may be rescued from oblivion, Briony's search for atonement turns out to be an attempt doomed from the start. While modernist writers still believed that the Truth can be glimpsed in fleeting moments of epiphany (cf. Proust's famous madeleine), postmodernism turns against this notion, claiming instead that all we can do in a post-metaphysical age, is arbitrate between different (conflicting) versions of truth and reality without ever arriving at a final, unchallengeable account.

Instead, she takes up a position that puts her in direct contact with the thoughts and feelings of the other. As Adamson puts it:

> The surrender of intellectual dominance and cognitive security [...] entails risk-taking, and a capability to be in mystery, without defensively reconstructing the world to fit one's desired shape or pattern. It involves imaginative excursiveness, a going-out of oneself, and also a letting-into oneself of things that may [...] surprise, shock, challenge, intensely disturb.[318]

In conclusion, we can state that Briony's crime of 1935 is a crime of the imagination, or rather, a crime caused by both an excess of imagination and a failure of imaginative projection into the other. In an article for the *Guardian* written on the occasion of the terror attacks of 11 September 2001 McEwan states:

> If the hijackers had been able to imagine themselves into the thoughts and feelings of the passengers, they would have been unable to proceed. It is hard to be cruel once you permit yourself to enter the mind of your victim. Imagining what it is like to be someone other than yourself is at the core of our humanity. It is the essence of compassion, and it is the beginning of morality.[319]

It is the latter kind of imagination that Briony spends the greatest part of her adult life seeking to acquire. Having mistakenly cast Robbie and Cecilia in a story that totally misinterpreted them, 77-year-old Briony sets out to retell the lovers' story with the "essence of compassion" she lacked as a thirteen-year-old girl and which, had she possessed it then, would have prevented her from committing her crime.

---

[318] Adamson, "Against Tidiness" 107.
[319] Ian McEwan, "Only love and then oblivion: Love was all they had to set against their murderers," *The Guardian Online* 16 Sept. 2001, 20 Mar. 2003 <http:// www. guardian.... ccrash/story/0,1300,552408,00.html>.

6. Journey's End: Achieving 'At-one-ment'?

6.1 Towards Greater Solidarity: Introducing the Liberal Ironist

Briony's literary debate with the voices of the other takes us back to Wayne C. Booth's concept of coduction and to our discussion of ethical criticism begun in chapter one of this paper. In fact, by imaginatively projecting herself into the lives of Robbie and Cecilia, by making room in her imagination for emotions, beliefs, and attachments that differ from her own, Briony "enters a process that is not mere argument for views already established, but a conversation, a kind of re-reading that is an essential part of [...] a continually shifting evaluation."[320] In recent interviews, Ian McEwan frequently referred to the novel as a medium of encounter and conversation, "a mental space which has a shape",[321] and an incentive for coduction, i.e. for the 'leading together' of different horizons and frameworks of belief. So for instance, in an interview conducted in September 2002, McEwan states:

> I think of all the art forms, the novel is supreme in giving us the possibility of inhabiting other minds. I think it does it better than drama; better than cinema. It's developed these elaborate conventions over three or four hundred years of representing not only mental states, but change, over time. [...] I think that 'other minds' is partly what the novel is about. If you saw the novel as I do in terms of being an exploration of human nature—an investigation of the human condition—then the main tool of that investigation has to be to demonstrate, to somehow give you, on the page, the sensual 'felt' feeling of what it is to be someone else.[322]

To experience "what it is to be someone else", however, I must assume responsibility for the other, I must, as Booth puts it, accept the "gambit" and enter into serious dialogue with the narrator, the implied author, or the characters of a novel and find out how their frameworks of belief join or conflict with mine.[323] Inhabiting another mind implies (temporarily) changing one's accustomed perspective or "habitat" and to enter into a space the singularity of which, even if it is produced by nothing more than a slight recasting of the familiar, reconfigures the *self*. Hence, Heinz Antor reminds us that even if we

---

[320] Booth, *Company* 75.
[321] Reynolds and Noakes, *Ian McEwan* 15.
[322] Koval, "Ian McEwan". Similarly, in an interview with *Bold Type* McEwan explained: "I value the word for its power to take a reader inside another person's mind, inside a character; we discover what it might be to be someone other than ourselves" *Bold Type*, "Interview".
[323] Booth, *Company* 135.

> [...] have come home again after our intellectual encounter with the other, [...] in the course of this challenge we have had an experience of defamiliarization and seen our patterns and frameworks from outside [...]. We have travelled and therefore our horizon has widened, even though it may not have changed fundamentally.[324]

In fact, we need not give up our accustomed frameworks or patterns of belief if we find that they are part of the story that makes the best sense for us, if they help us give a best account of our lives. Still, if we want to avoid intellectual rigidity, narrow-mindedness, snobbishness, and self-satisfaction, we do well to accept the challenge of alterity and give the other "an open and fair appraisal"[325] rather than reject it unthinkingly from the outset.

The ability and willingness to imaginatively project oneself into other people, to suspend one's own belief and to give the other the benefit of the doubt at least, is the prerequisite of human solidarity. Solidarity, understood in the sense of responsibility for or obligation to other human beings, is strongest, however, as Rorty observes, "when those with whom solidarity is expressed are thought of as 'one of us', where 'us' means something smaller than and more local than the human race."[326] Indeed, we are more likely to feel solidarity with people who are similar to us, who share with us what Wilfrid Sellars calls "we-intentions",[327] who are, for instance, fellow Catholics, fellow citizens, members of the same gender, or the same family. In contrast, people who are dissimilar in a way that strikes us as salient, form the great mass of "they" in our lives. With "them" imaginative identification is not as easily possibly as with "us" and hence our sense of solidarity or moral obligation is much weaker when "they" are concerned.

As we have already stated before, novels like *The Child in Time*, *Black Dogs*, *Enduring Love*, and *Atonement* do not filter conflicting ideas, concepts, or beliefs through an authoritative voice that neatly resolves all ambiguities and offers the reader a fool-proof master version of the Truth. Rather, they invite us to imaginatively partake in opposing stories of the *self* and the world, to formulate and revise opinions as we take in the novels' "data". Looking at the world through the eyes of characters or narrators as different as Briony, Robbie, Jed, Joe, Bernard, June, Jeremy, Julie, or Stephen, we encounter diversity in a way that encourages a broad tolerance of many views and induces us to transform dissimilar "strangers" into "acquaintances". In the course of this enterprise, we are enticed to re-assess our previous we-intentions and to "*create* a more expansive sense of solidarity than we presently have."[328] In *Black Dogs*,

---

[324] Antor, "Ethics" 72.
[325] Antor, "Ethics" 73.
[326] Rorty, *Contingency* 191.
[327] Rorty, *Contingency* 190.
[328] Rorty, *Contingency* 196.

Jeremy refers to this enlarged notion of tolerance when he asks June the rhetorical question: "Don't you think the world should be able to accommodate your way of looking at things and Bernard's? [...] Isn't it diversity what (sic!) makes a civilisation?" (*BD* 51).

Solidarity in modern democratic societies, Rorty explains, is neither "a matter of sharing a common truth or a common goal", nor are we united with the rest of the human species by some universal, inborn ur-vocabulary of human solidarity, by the "recognition of a core self, the human essence, in all human beings."[329] What can unite us with people who are very different from us, however, is the awareness that we share the "common selfish hope, [...] that one's world [...] will not be destroyed"[330] and that, as "embodied, finite, [...] and emotive"[331] beings, we are susceptible "to pain and in particular to that special sort of pain which the brutes do not share with the humans – humiliation."[332] Rorty calls the kind of person who can imaginatively identify with the pain and suffering of fellow human beings, but who does not believe in an intrinsic, shared humanity, a "liberal ironist."[333] As an ironist, this person has given up all "ambition of transcendence"[334] and does not commit the "ontological fallacy"[335] of setting up his framework of belief as the framework *tout court*. Rather, he conceives of his frameworks or patterns of belief as *foci imaginarii*,[336] as creations or inventions, which - though not offering him access to some ultimate Truth or higher Reality - are concepts he needs in order to gain orientation in moral space. In contrast to the "mere" ironist, the liberal ironist believes that "cruelty is the worst thing we do";[337] he is convinced that solidarity is achieved via "the imaginative ability to see strange people as fellow sufferers."[338]

Aware of the pain and humiliation caused by "telling other people that the metaphysical language they talk is futile, obsolete, and powerless",[339] liberal ironists refrain from forcing their notion of contingency on people who do not share their ironist outlook on the world. Hence, liberal ironists distinguish between a private irony that allows them to redescribe the world and other people in terms which have nothing to do with their attitude towards other

---

[329] Rorty, *Contingency* 192.
[330] Rorty, *Contingency* 92.
[331] Benhabib, *Situating* 50.
[332] Rorty, *Contingency* 92.
[333] Rorty, *Contingency* xv.
[334] Rorty, *Objectivity* 12.
[335] Antor, "Ethics" 75.
[336] Rorty, *Contingency* 195. Cf. also: Antor, "Ethics" 78.
[337] Rorty, *Contingency* xv.
[338] Rorty, *Contingency* xvi.
[339] Rorty, *Contingency* 90.

people's "actual or possible suffering"[340] and a public liberalism which acknowledges the ways in which an ironist vocabulary - if publicly used - may hurt or humiliate other people. Joe, at the beginning of *Enduring Love*, is an ironist who lacks the imaginative dimension of the liberal. After the ballooning accident, for example, when he and Parry meet in the field where Logan's body is sitting, Joe turns down Parry's offer to pray with him with the following explanation: "Because, my friend, no one's listening. There is no one up there" (*EL* 26). As a private ironist, Joe is free to renounce the presence of a higher Being, he is also free to decline Parry's offer as it would make no sense for him to address a Being whose existence he denies. Joe's cruelty, his failure of imaginative projection, lies in the *way* he refuses Parry's offer, in the way he (mis)uses his private ironist vocabulary to publicly and humiliatingly redescribe Parry's metaphysical world-view.

In contrast to Joe, 77-year-old Briony is able to distinguish between private irony and public liberalism. Sixty years of guilt have taught her to imagine the pain and suffering that can be inflicted on other people by making one's private interpretations and (re)descriptions of them public. In the final version of her story, Briony does not only declare her solidarity with Robbie and Cecilia by imaginatively projecting herself into their feelings, but she extends her solidarity, her awareness of human suffering, to her readers: While "[a]ll the preceding drafts were pitiless" (*A* 370) in so far as they denied the lovers a happy reunion, in the final draft of 1999 Robbie and Cecilia "survive to love" (*A* 371). By ending her novel on this benign note, Briony - apart from giving the lovers the happiness they were denied in "real" life - tries to spare her imagined readers the painful experience of reading a story that frustrates their metaphysical yearning for a meaningful universe in which all fates are resolved and suffering is part of a greater telic plan that leads to happiness. Thus, Briony consciously rejects the possibility of telling her readers that Robbie and Cecilia died before they had a chance to see each other again after the fatal summer's day of 1935:

> How could that [the death of Robbie and Cecilia] constitute an ending? What sense of hope or satisfaction could a reader draw from such an account? Who would want to believe that they never met again, never fulfilled their love? Who would want to believe that, except in the service of the bleakest realism? (*A* 371)

As readers of the novel *Atonement* written by the flesh and blood author Ian McEwan, however, Briony's reflections concerning the ending of her story are not withheld from us. By appending a coda in which Briony muses about the effect of the chosen ending of her novel, McEwan reminds us of the fact that

---

[340] Rorty, *Contingency* 91.

human solidarity and patterns of meaning are created and not found, that empathy is not given to us with birth, but developed through experience.

6.2 Tying Knots and Closing Questions?

In the preceding chapter we argued with Richard Rorty that "a belief can still regulate action [...] among people who are quite aware that this belief is caused by nothing deeper than contingent [...] circumstances."[341] We introduced the liberal ironist as a person who is aware of the contingency of his beliefs and attachments, who creates *foci imaginarii* instead of searching for universal Truths, who has abandoned "the discourse, the vocabulary, of objectivity and work[s] instead towards expanding human solidarity."[342] The liberal ironist's acknowledgement of the contingency of his own most central beliefs and desires and his eagerness to continually extend his we-intentions to people previously thought of as "they", implies a potential open-mindedness, a readiness to seek

> as much imaginative acquaintance with alternative [...] vocabularies as possible, not just for [his] own edification, but in order to understand the actual and possible humiliation of the people who use these alternative [...] vocabularies.[343]

Given his intellectual open-mindedness, his constant revision of opinions, and his continuous redescription of him*self*, how can the liberal ironist ever achieve 'at-one-ment'? In other words, how can a liberal ironist feel that his life choices and convictions are 'at one' with what he perceives of as his *self*, if this *self* is unmasked as a mental construct that is continuously being redescribed?

To answer these questions, we must consider the ultimate aim or goal of redescription in the ironist's life. Rorty explains that the ironist hopes - by continual redescription of himself and of the world he inhabits - to make the best *self* for himself that he can.[344] Hence, although he denies the existence of a divine or essential *self*, the ironist continues to formulate coherent stories of the *self*, using redescription to turn himself into a person whose mind gradually grows "larger and stronger and more interesting by the addition of new options – new candidates for belief and desire, phrased in new vocabularies."[345] Redescription, rather than preventing 'at-one-ment', thus turns out to be the very means by which ironists (re)create themselves and adapt to the changing

---

[341] Rorty, *Contingency* 189.
[342] Brandom, *Rorty and his Critics* xi.
[343] Rorty, *Contingency* 92.
[344] Rorty, *Contingency* 80.
[345] Rorty, *Objectivity* 14.

contexts of their lives. 'At-one-ment', in the ironist's sense, is no static concept, but a dynamic one, changing with changing beliefs and convictions.

However, to experience 'at-one-ment', to feel that our current choices and convictions are 'at one' with what we conceive of as our present *self*, we must place some restriction on the potential openness in our lives. In fact, there must exist some resting places or closures inside the dynamic process of redescription if we are to experience and savour the sense of wholeness and belonging that characterises the good life. Constant openness or a blind acceptance of anything new that comes our way would make us lose our bearings in moral space and leave us unable to distinguish between redescriptions that help us grow larger and stronger and redescriptions that cripple. Permanent closure, on the other hand, breeds intellectual arrogance and fosters an attitude of foundationalist narrow-mindedness that is strikingly opposed to the ideal of a liberal society in which conflicting and incommensurable values are played off against one another in an ongoing discourse. Heinz Antor introduces the image of the many-storied building to stress the necessary interplay of stasis and dynamics, openness and closure, travelling and arrival in our lives. He states that

> [w]e can have the dynamics of an infinite succession of static stages, like steps of an ever-spiralling staircase. The staircase may even have landings where we can and need to rest for some time before we look out for the other and go on to the next floor. But we should not stay on a landing forever and adopt it as our permanent intellectual platform.[346]

Similarly, in his defence of ethical criticism, Wayne C. Booth criticises the elevation of openness to a universal value by raising four major objections against "blanket attacks" on closure in fictional narrative.[347] First and foremost, Booth claims that "no literary work of any consequence, in anybody's view, is entirely open."[348] He posits that even if there existed a totally open work consisting of nothing but arbitrarily arranged cryptic symbols, "every reader would automatically try to close it in order to make something of it [...]."[349] In fact, as avid pattern-builders, "we are unable to resist making sense of whatever data we encounter, even if the data are [...] random."[350] Total openness, Booth expounds, "is total entropy – and hence total apathy for the reader."[351] Thus, in order for a work of fiction to interest the reader and to make possible some kind

---

[346] Antor, "Ethics" 82.
[347] Booth, *Company* 60ff.
[348] Wayne C. Booth, "Are Narrative Choices Subject to Ethical Criticism?" *Reading Narrative. Form, Ethics, Ideology*, ed. James Phelan (Columbus: Ohio State UP, 1989) 65.
[349] Booth, *Company* 62.
[350] Booth, "Narrative Choices" 65.
[351] Booth, "Narrative Choices" 67.

of (ethical) gain, it must combine "specific closures with specific openings."[352] Secondly, Booth proceeds, we must distinguish between different degrees of openness encountered in literary works.[353] An author can, for example, leave some questions open and engage his readers in the ethical enterprise of trying to work out answers for themselves or in (controversial) discussions with other readers; at the same time, however, he must definitively close off some possibilities of interpretation. Thirdly, Booth points out that readers vary with regard to their social, historical, or cultural background and that it would be presumptuous to claim that what every reader in every epoch needs most is the experience of openness and that "there are no other ethical effects that for some readers in some circumstances might be more valuable."[354] Finally, Booth argues that leaving questions open "is never an end in itself but always either a side effect or a means to some other end."[355] Thus, he elaborates, in its most questionable form, openness may be used as "a means to the end of seeming up-to-date: originally modern but now always 'post-modern' or 'post-structuralist' or 'post-deconstructionist.' "[356] At its most profound, however, openness can serve as a means of providing a genuine encounter with the other.[357]

The four novels discussed in this paper combine a certain degree of openness or indeterminacy with clear determinacies or closures. Reading McEwan's novels, we keep the company of texts that offer us some conceptual toeholds but which, at the same time, remind us of the indeterminacy and unpredictability of life in a post-metaphysical world. In *The Child in Time*, for instance, Stephen and Julie's rekindled love and the birth of the new baby constitute a "happy ending" that satisfactorily ties up the loose ends of what we may call the "love story strand" of the novel. The infinite possibilities of Thelma's quantum magic are reduced to one single version of reality in which Stephen and Julie fully acknowledge the loss of Kate and find solace in their love for each other and for their new child. Still, at the end of the novel, not *all* questions are answered and not *all* loose ends are tied up. The gender of the baby, for instance, is not revealed and - most importantly - Kate remains lost and we are none the wiser with regard to her abductor or whereabouts than we were at the beginning of the novel. As we are neither presented with a "body" nor with a criminal, the "detective story strand" of *The Child in Time* remains untied. By subverting the expectations which the reader brings to the genre of the whodunnit, McEwan reminds us that there exists no final Truth and that no amount of careful pattern-building can completely ward off the impact of

---

[352] Booth, *Company* 63.
[353] Booth, "Narrative Choices" 69.
[354] Booth, *Company* 68.
[355] Booth, "Narrative Choices" 72.
[356] Booth, *Company* 69.
[357] Booth, *Company* 69.

contingency in our lives. In a world where change and arbitrariness are omnipresent, personal attachments constitute an empowering but fragile resting place. Hence, even as Julie and Stephen are enjoying their newfound intimacy in the minutes after the baby's arrival, their private world is slowly being invaded by the great openness "outside":

> Beyond the bed was the window through which they could see the moon sinking into a gap in the pines. Directly above the moon was a planet. It was Mars, Julie said. It was a reminder of the harsh world. For now, however, they were immune, it was before the beginning of time, and they lay watching planet and moon descend through a sky that was turning blue. [...] 'Well?' Julie said. 'A girl or a boy?' And it was in acknowledgement of the world they were about to rejoin, and into which they hoped to take their love, that she reached under the covers and felt. (*CT* 222-223)

In *Black Dogs*, a kind of temporal closure is achieved when we learn that the huge dogs of June's metaphysical encounter were guard dogs of the Gestapo and hence neither mystical beasts nor figments of her imagination. The different explanations of the animals' presence on the country path are reduced to one rational explanation. However, at the end of the novel, the dogs run off not as real animals, but as "spirit hounds, incarnations" (*BD* 173), into a desolate landscape that is part southern France, part a dream, and from there "they will return to haunt us, somewhere in Europe, in another time" (*BD* 174). Thus, not all ambiguities are resolved and the private world of happy family life, the "hearth" Jeremy has been searching for all his life, turns out to be a precarious resting place, endangered by some unspecified human evil, incorporated in the form of the retreating dogs. Still, for the time being Jeremy, like Stephen and Julie at the end of *The Child in Time*, is able to rest and appreciate the happiness he has found, even if this happiness is tainted by the awareness that he owes his home, his wife, his family to contingency, to the world's "historical and personal forces, the huge and tiny currents, that had to align and combine" (*BD* 173) to make him the man he is.

At first glance, *Enduring Love* seems to close more questions than the other three novels discussed in this paper. True to the genre conventions of the thriller a mounting suspense is created that revolves around the danger Jed Parry poses in his delusional state. Towards the end of the novel, when Parry takes Clarissa hostage and Joe overpowers him in a traditional climactic confrontation, tension peaks and is finally released: Parry is institutionalised and Joe is vindicated as a reliable narrator. As an epistemological thriller and a love story, however, *Enduring Love* provides no permanent closure. As Clarissa points out in her letter to Joe, "your being right is not a simple matter" (*EL* 216). We saw that in the course of the novel, Joe's scientific world-view suffers severe blows and, helpful though his stubborn rationality proves to be in the chaos of being stalked by Parry, it does not endear him to his girlfriend. Hence, as we reach the end of the novel, we do not know whether Joe and Clarissa will finally reunite, if they will be able to summon the tolerance and open-mindedness needed to accept that any story is nothing but a partial retelling of events.

In *Atonement*, 77-year-old Briony prefers the "happy ending" of Robbie and Cecilia's love story to a bleak account of their unfulfilled love. Leaving all knots untied, all fates unresolved, she realises, is against the grain of human nature; it would, as Briony puts it, offer neither "hope [n]or satisfaction" (*A* 371). In fact, hope is what we need to go on searching for the good life in a world where contingency constantly threatens the unity of the *self*. Without the indefatigable hope that life will improve, that our present suffering will give way to happiness, satisfaction, and a sense of 'at-one-ment', life would be bereft of meaning. The disappointment that we - as readers of Ian McEwan's novel - experience when we realise that Briony has made up the greatest part of Robbie's and Cecilia's story, is directly related to our yearning for closures that make sense, that create the illusion of a meaningful *telos*, of life having grown richer and fuller. Still, to retain hope, to go on believing that "life will eventually be freer, less cruel, more leisured, richer in goods and experiences"[358] we cannot permanently close ourselves off against change and contingency. To move towards a fuller and richer life, we need to be flexible in the face of the unknown or unfamiliar.

---

[358] Rorty, *Contingency* 86.

7. Conclusion

In our discussion of storytelling and the concept of the *self* in Ian McEwan's *The Child in Time, Black Dogs, Enduring Love,* and *Atonement* one central assumption is borne out time and again: We find that despite the contingency of all stories of the *self* and the world, despite the absence of metaphysical foundations, and despite the precarious nature of all attachments and frameworks of belief, the quest for the good life, for meaning, purpose, and 'at-one-ment', constitutes an integral, ineradicable part of the characters' lives. We stated that as human agents or *selves*, we exist in a space of "inescapable questions"[359] about who and what we are, about where we are and where we are going, and that in order to live a good life rather than a mere life, we need to answer these questions for ourselves.

We furthermore argued that the quest for the good life is a narrative quest directed towards a *telos* of fullness or wholeness, towards a coherent story that makes sense of our past, present and future. As Taylor puts it, "we want the future to 'redeem' the past, to make it part of a life story which has sense or purpose, to take it up to a meaningful unity."[360] What constitutes a meaningful story, however, depends on our individual outlook on life, on our unique perspective on a world of conflicting choices and explanatory patterns. We claimed that McEwan's protagonists arrive at best accounts of their lives - i.e. at stories of the *self* that come closest to explaining the phenomena encountered in the world and make sense "across the whole range of both explanatory and life uses",[361] by living through transitions that prove error-reducing and are thus conceived of by the characters as an epistemic gain.

We conceded, however, that there is more to a best account than a reasoned transition from one explanatory pattern to another. In order to accept *this* hypergood rather than *that* or to turn towards *this* framework of belief rather than to *that* at *this* point in our lives, we need to be moved by it, we need to feel some kind of emotional pull in addition to the sober conviction that a certain story of the *self* and the world provides the best answer to the pressing epistemological and ontological questions which we cannot avoid. We introduced Martha Nussbaum's cognitive-evaluative theory of emotions which centres around the assumption that emotions - though often experienced as uprooting, tumultuous, and beyond rational understanding - enter intelligently into our perceptions and beliefs and thus ineliminably contribute to our individual well-being. Nussbaum's grasp of the complex, *eudaimonistic* nature of emotions may well be instrumental in bringing about a new turn within the

---

[359] Taylor, *Sources* 41.
[360] Taylor, *Sources* 51.
[361] Taylor, *Sources* 58.

ethics debate, leading to the reassessment of a whole range of works of fiction that explore emotions such as love, grief, guilt, compassion, and fear.

We submitted McEwan's latest novel *Atonement* to an "emotional" reading, focussing on Briony's feelings of guilt and her growing compassion for *selves* apart from her own. Most importantly, we claimed that "emotions typically have a connection to the imagination" and that "this imagining is best understood as a vehicle for making a eudaimonistic connection with the object."[362] Briony's imaginative debate with the voices of the other took us back to the interplay between *self* and other discussed in chapter three. We introduced Richard Rorty's liberal ironist as a person who uses a vocabulary that does not put emphasis on objective Truth, but on *self*-creation and imagination. Aware of the contingency of his beliefs and attachments, the liberal ironist adheres to *foci imaginarii*; he continuously creates and re-creates him*self* to meet the new situations he encounters. Sensible of the potentially cruel nature of public redescription, he restricts his redescribing activities to the private domain of his life.

With Rorty's liberal ironist we introduced a postmodern character who has overcome the metaphysical project of knowing the Truth, but who - unlike Nietzsche and his ironist successors - does not believe in the total autonomy of the *self*. The liberal ironist is conscious of "the egocentric character of the aesthetics of self-creation and therefore wants to see it supplemented by an aesthetics of solidarity."[363] By offering us antirepresentationalist accounts of diverging interpretations of the *self* and the world, by being keenly aware of human pain and suffering, and by presenting us with sympathetic, imaginative portrayals of the flawed, suffering, disorientated characters in his novels, Ian McEwan proves to be an ironist author who is also a liberal. In Rorty's jargon, McEwan is "able to separate the question 'Do you believe and desire what we believe and desire?' from the question 'Are you suffering?' ", he is able to "distinguish public from private questions, questions about pain from questions about the point of human life, the domain of the liberal from the domain of the ironist."[364]

As a liberal ironist, Ian McEwan offers us insights into a culture where different world-views are played off against one another, where we-intentions are continuously enlarged, and where the decentred *selves* of a disenchanted age do not follow the deconstructionist imperative to "[w]ithdraw. Abnegate. Give up. Get out of the vicious circle",[365] but stay inside an ongoing discourse of values, narratively creating and recreating them*selves* and searching for new

---

[362] Nussbaum, *Upheavals* 65.
[363] Bredella, "Aesthetics" 50.
[364] Rorty, *Contingency* 198.
[365] Hillis J. Miller, "Is There an Ethics of Reading?" *Reading Narrative: Form, Ethics, Ideology*, ed. James Phelan (Columbus: Ohio State UP, 1989) 99.

(provisional) centres of meaning. We are in favour of such a democratic "poeticized culture",[366] a liberal utopia, which, by appreciating that all touchstones of truth are cultural artefacts, "take[s] as its goal the creation of ever more various and multicoloured artefacts."[367] Only a culture that has abandoned the discourse of objectivity and works instead towards enlarging solidarity is tolerant enough to invite all moral agents to create them*selves* without curbing individual freedom and falling back upon restrictive universalist master narratives.[368]

In a postmodern poeticised culture, imaginative literature represents an indispensable mode of acquainting us with new ways of living the good life and of furthering "moral conversations in which we exercise the reversibility of perspectives by representing to ourselves imaginatively the many perspectives [of the other]."[369] Keeping the company of Ian McEwan's *The Child in Time*, *Black Dogs*, *Enduring Love*, and *Atonement*, we are tempted to exercise this reversibility of perspectives, to revise our own *self*-accounts and to maybe come up with a new story of the *self* that, until further revision, gives us a sense of having come closer to some kind of 'at-one-ment' in our lives.

---

[366] Rorty, *Contingency* 53.

[367] Rorty, *Contingency* 54.

[368] Note that the concept of the utopian poeticised culture envisaged by Rorty remains open to interpretation and re-interpretation like all other cultural artefacts and systems of belief. Arguing against the setting up of master narratives entails that we remain aware of the danger of setting up a liberal ironist, democratic culture as a new master narrative.

[369] Benhabib, *Situating* 54.

8. Works Cited

Adamson, Jane. "Against Tidiness. Literature and/versus Moral Philosophy." *Renegotiating Ethics in Literature, Philosophy, and Theory*. Ed. Jane Adamson, Richard Freadman, and David Parker. Cambridge: Cambridge UP, 1998. 84-110.

Antor, Heinz. "Ethical Plurivocity, or: The Pleasures and Rewards of Reading." *Text – Culture – Reception. Cross- Cultural Aspects of English Studies*. Ed. Rüdiger Ahrens and Heinz Antor. Heidelberg: C. Winter, 1992. 27-46.

---. "The Ethics of Criticism in the Age After Value." *Why Literature Matters: Theories and Functions of Literature*. Ed. Rüdiger Ahrens and Laurenz Volkmann. Heidelberg: C. Winter, 1996. 65-85.

---. "The Arts, the Sciences, and the Making of Meaning: Tom Stoppard's *Arcadia* as a Post-Structuralist Play." *Anglia* 116 (1998): 326-354.

---. "Unreliable Narration and (Dis-)Orientation in the Postmodern Neo-Gothic Novel: Reflections on Patrick McGrath's *The Grotesque* (1989)." *Erzählen und Erzähltheorie im 20. Jahrhundert*. Anglistische Forschungen 294. Ed. Jörg Helbig. Heidelberg: C. Winter, 2001. 357-382.

Attridge, Derek. "Innovation, Literature, Ethics: Relating to the Other." *PMLA* 114 (1999): 20-31.

Begley, Adam. "The Art of Fiction CLXXIII." *The Paris Review* 162 (2002). 10 Apr. 2003 <http:// www.parisreview.com/tpr162/mcewan1.html>.

Bell, Michael. "The Metaphysics of Modernism." *The Cambridge Companion to Modernism*. Ed. Michael Levenson. Cambridge: Cambridge UP, 1999. 9-32.

Benhabib, Seyla. *Situating the Self: Gender, Community and Postmodernism in Contemporary Ethics*. Cambridge: Cambridge UP, 1992.

Bewes, Timothy. "What is Philosophical Honesty in Postmodern Literature?" *New Literary History* 31 (2000): 421-434.

Bold Type. "An Interview with Ian McEwan." *Bold Type* 2.9 (1998). 10 Dec. 2002 <http://www.randomhouse.com/boldtype/0398/mcewan/ interview. html>.

Booth, Wayne C. *The Rhetoric of Fiction*. 1961. Chicago: University of Chicago Press, 1965.

---. *The Company We Keep: An Ethics of Fiction*. Berkeley: University of California Press, 1988.

---. "Are Narrative Choices Subject to Ethical Criticism?" *Reading Narrative. Form, Ethics, Ideology*. Ed. James Phelan. Columbus: Ohio State UP, 1989. 57-78.

Brandom, Robert, ed. *Rorty and His Critics*. Malden, Mass.: Blackwell, 2000.

Bredella, Lothar. "Aesthetics and Ethics: Incommensurable, Identical or Conflicting?" *Ethics and Aesthetics: The Moral Turn of Postmodernism.* Ed. Gerhard Hoffmann, and Alfred Hornung. Heidelberg: C. Winter, 1996. 29-51.
Bruner, Jerome. *Making Stories: Law, Literature, Life.* New York: Farrar, 2002.
Bußmann, Hadumod. *Lexikon der Sprachwissenschaft.* Kröners Taschenausgabe Bd. 452. Stuttgart: Kröner, 1990.
Cahoone, Lawrence, ed. *From Modernism to Postmodernism. An Anthology.* 1996. Oxford: Blackwell, 2000.
Chomsky, Noam. *Knowledge of Language: Its Nature, Origin and Use.* New York: Praeger, 1986.
Clayton, Lay. "The Absent Signifier: Historical Narrative and the Abstract Subject." *Ethics and the Subject.* Ed. Karl Simms. Amsterdam: Rodopi, 1997. 77-83.
Connor, Steven. *Theory and Cultural Value.* 1988. London: Blackwell, 1992.
---. "After Cultural Value: Ecology, Ethics, Aesthetics." *Ethics and Aesthetics: The Moral Turn of Postmodernism.* Ed. Gerhard Hoffmann and Alfred Hornung. Heidelberg: C. Winter, 1996. 1-12.
Cordle, Daniel. *Postmodern Postures: Literature, Science and the Two Cultures Debate.* Aldershot: Ashgate, 1999.
Cordner, Christopher. "F.R. Leavis and the Moral in Literature." *On Literary Theory and Philosophy: A Cross- Disciplinary Encounter.* Ed. Richard Freadman and Lloyd Reinhardt. London: Macmillan, 1991. 60-81.
Cuddon, J.A. *The Penguin Dictionary of Literary Terms and Literary Theory.* 3rd ed. London: Penguin, 1992.
Davidson, Donald. *Subjective, Intersubjective, Objective.* Oxford: Oxford UP, 2001.
Day, Aidan. *Romanticism.* London: Routledge, 1996.
Delrez, Marc. "Escape into Innocence: Ian McEwan and the Nightmare of History." *Ariel- A Review of International English Literature* 26.2 (1995): 7-23.
Diamond, Cora. "Martha Nussbaum and the Need for Novels." *Renegotiating Ethics in Literature, Philosophy, and Theory.* Ed. Jane Adamson, Richard Freadman, and David Parker. Cambridge: Cambridge UP, 1998. 39-64.
Docherty, Thomas. *Alterities. Criticism, History, Representation.* Oxford: Clarendon, 1996.
Eakin, Paul John. *How Our Lives Become Stories: Making Selves.* Ithaka: Cornell UP, 1999.
Edwards, Paul. "Time, Romanticism, Modernism and Moderation in Ian McEwan's *The Child in Time.*" *English* 44 (1995): 41-55.
Finney, Brian. "Briony's Stand Against Oblivion: Ian McEwan's *Atonement.*" *Brian Finney's Webside.* 2002. Dept. of English, California State

University. 3 May 2003. <http://www.csulb.edu/~bhfinney/McEwan.html>.

Fokkema, Aleid. *Postmodern Characters. A Study of Characterization in British and American Postmodern Fiction*. Amsterdam: Rodopi, 1991.

Foucault, Michel. *The History of Sexuality: An Introduction*. Trans. Robert Hurley. Vol. 1. London: Penguin, 1978.

---. *The History of Sexuality: The Use of Pleasure*. 1984. Trans. Robert Hurley. Vol. 2. London: Penguin, 1992.

Freadman, Richard, and Seumas Miller. *Re-Thinking Theory: A Critique of Contemporary Literary Theory and an Alternative Account*. Cambridge: Cambridge UP, 1992.

Gardiner, Michael. "Alterity and Ethics: A Dialogical Perspective." *Theory, Culture and Society* 13 (1996): 121-143.

Garner, Dwight. "The Salon Interview: Ian McEwan." *Salon. Com*. 31 Mar. 1998. 4 Feb. 2003 <http://dir.salon.com/books/int/1998/03/cov_si_31 int.html>.

Gibson, Andrew. *Postmodernity, Ethics and the Novel*. London: Routledge, 1999.

Grabes, Herbert. "Ethics, Aesthetics, and Alterity." *Ethics and Aesthetics: The Moral Turn of Postmodernism*. Ed. Gerhard Hoffmann and Alfred Hornung. Heidelberg: C. Winter, 1996. 13-29.

Gras, Vernon W. "The Recent Ethical Turn in Literary Studies." *Mitteilungen des Verbandes Deutscher Anglisten* 4.2 (1993): 30-41.

Haines, Simon. "Deepening the Self. The Language of Ethics and the Language of Literature." *Renegotiating Ethics in Literature, Philosophy, and Theory*. Ed. Jane Adamson, Richard Freadman, and David Parker. Cambridge: Cambridge UP, 1998. 221-238.

Herrnstein Smith, Barbara. *Contingencies of Value. Alternative Perspectives for Critical Theory*. Cambridge, Mass.: Harvard UP, 1988.

Holquist, Michael. *Dialogism: Bakhtin and his World*. London, New York: Routledge, 1990.

Hügli, Anton, and Poul Lübcke. 1991. *Philosophielexikon. Personen und Begriffe der abendländischen Philosophie von der Antike bis zur Gegenwart*. Hamburg: Rowohlt, 2001.

Hunt, Adam. "Ian McEwan." *B&A: New Fiction* 21 (1996): 47-50.

Hutcheon, Linda. *The Politics of Postmodernism*. London: Routledge, 1989.

Hutto, J.D.D. "The Story of the Self: The Narrative Basis of Self-Development." *Ethics and the Subject*. Ed. Karl Simms. Amsterdam: Rodopi, 1997. 61-75.

Iser, Wolfgang. *Der Akt des Lesens*. München: UTB, 1976.

Kellaway, Kate. "At Home with his Worries." *The Observer* 16 Sept. 2001. 10 Dec. 2002 <http://www.books.guardian...iction/story/0,6000,552557,00. html>.
Kershner, Brandon R. "Mikhail Bakhtin and Bakhtinian Criticism." *Introducing Literary Theories: A Guide and Glossary*. Ed. Julian Wolfreys. Edinburgh: Edinburgh UP, 2001. 19-32.
Kiernan, Ryan. *Ian McEwan. Writers and Their Work*. Ed. Isabel Armstrong. Plymouth: Northcote House; London: The British Council, 1994.
Koval, Ramona. "Ian McEwan." *Books and Writing*. 22 Sept. 2002. 23 May 2003 <http://www.abc.net.au/rn/bwriting/stories/s679422.htm>.
Lamarque, Peter, and Haugom Olson Stein. *Truth, Fiction and Literature*. Oxford: Clarendon, 1994.
Langford, Paul. "The Eighteenth Century." *The Oxford History of Britain*. 1983. Ed. Kenneth O. Morgan. Oxford: Oxford UP, 1993. 399-469.
Lewis, Peter. "Ian McEwan." *Contemporary Novelists*. Ed. D.L. Kirkpatrick. London: St. James, 1986. 590-592.
MacIntyre, Alasdair. *After Virtue*. 1981. London: Duckworth, 1985.
---. "The Claims of After Virtue." *The MacIntyre Reader*. Ed. Kevin Knight. Cambridge: Polity, 1998. 69-72.
Malcolm, David. *Understanding Ian McEwan*. Columbia: University of South Carolina Press, 2002.
McEwan, Ian. *The Child in Time*. 1987. London: Vintage, 2001.
---. *Black Dogs*. 1992. London: Vintage, 1998.
---. *Enduring Love*. 1997. London: Vintage, 1998.
---. *Atonement*. 2001. London: Vintage, 2002.
---. "Only love and then oblivion: Love was all they had to set against their murderers." *The Guardian Online* 16 Sept. 2001. 20 Mar. 2003 <http://www.guardian....ccrash/story/ 0,1300,552408,00.html>.
Miller, J. Hillis. "Is There an Ethics of Reading?" *Reading Narrative: Form, Ethics, Ideology*. Ed. James Phelan. Columbus: Ohio State UP, 1989. 79-101.
Nünning, Ansgar. "Zwischen der realistischen Erzähltradition und der experimentellen Poetik des Postmodernismus: Erscheinungsformen und Entwicklungstendenzen des englischen Romans seit dem zweiten Weltkrieg aus gattungstheoretischer Perspektive." *Eine andere Geschichte der englischen Literatur: Epochen, Gattungen und Teilgebiete im Überblick*. Ed. Monika Fludernik und Ansgar Nünning. WVT-Handbücher zum literaturwissenschaftlichen Studium 2. Trier: WVT, 1996. 213-235.
---. *Der englische Roman des 20. Jahrhunderts*. Uni-Wissen Anglistik, Amerikanistik. Stuttgart: Klett, 1998.

Nussbaum, Martha C. "Perceptive Equilibrium: Literary Theory and Ethical Theory." *The Future of Literary Theory*. Ed. Ralph Cohen. London: Routledge, 1989. 58-85.

---. *Upheavals of Thought: The Intelligence of Emotions*. Cambridge: Cambridge UP, 2001.

Parker, David. "The Turn to Ethics in the 1990s." Introduction. *Renegotiating Ethics in Literature, Philosophy, and Theory*. Ed. Jane Adamson, Richard Freadman, and David Parker. Cambridge: Cambridge UP, 1998: 1-17.

Pedot, Richard. "Une narration en quête de son sujet: Chemin de l'écriture et écriture du chemin dans *Black Dogs* de Ian McEwan." *Études Britanniques Contemporaines* 11 (1997): 67-75.

Reynolds, Margaret, and Jonathan Noakes. *Ian McEwan: The Essential Guide*. London: Vintage, 2002.

Reynolds, Oliver. "A Master of Accidents." *Times Literary Supplement*, 12 Sept. 1997: 12.

Ricks, Christopher. "Adolescence and After - An Interview with Ian McEwan." *Listener* 101 (1979): 526-527.

Rorty, Richard. *Contingency, Irony and Solidarity*. Cambridge: Cambridge UP, 1989.

---. *Objectivity, Relativism, and Truth*. Cambridge: Cambridge UP, 1991.

Schlaeger, Jürgen. "Who's Afraid of Ian McEwan?" *Beyond Borders: Redefining Generic and Ontological Boundaries*. Ed. Ramón Plo-Alastrúe and María Jesús Martínez-Alfaro. Heidelberg: C.Winter, 2002. 185-195.

Schoeck, Eric. "An Interview with Ian McEwan." *Capitola Book Café*. 16 Feb. 1998. 10 Dec. 2002 <http://www.capitolabookcafe.com/andrea/ mcewan.html>.

Siebers, Tobin. *The Ethics of Criticism*. Ithaca: Cornell UP, 1988.

Slay, Jack, Jr. *Ian McEwan*. New York: Twayne; London: Prentice Hall, 1996.

Smith, Nicholas H. "Contingency and Self-Identity: Taylor's Hermeneutics vs. Rorty's Postmodernism." *Theory, Culture & Society* 13.2 (1996): 105-120.

Soper, Kate. "Postmodernism, Subjectivity and the Question of Value." *Principled Positions: Postmodernism and the Rediscovery of Value*. Ed. J. Squires. London: Lawrence & Wishart, 1993. 17-30.

Swift, Graham. *Waterland*. 1983. London: Picador, 1992.

Taylor, Charles. *Sources of the Self: The Making of the Modern Identity*. Cambridge: Cambridge UP, 1989.

Waugh, Patricia. "Revising the Two Cultures Debate: Science, Literature and Value." *The Arts and Sciences of Criticism*. David Fuller and Patricia Waugh. Oxford: Oxford UP, 1999. 33-59.

Welsch, Wolfgang. *Unsere Postmoderne Moderne*. Berlin: Akademischer Verlag, 1997.

Wright, Derek. "New Physics, Old Metaphysics: Quantum and Quotidian in Ian McEwan's *The Child in Time.*" *Revista alicantina de estudios ingleses* 10 (1997): 221-233.

ANGLO-AMERIKANISCHE STUDIEN - ANGLO-AMERICAN STUDIES

Herausgegeben von
Rüdiger Ahrens (Würzburg) und Kevin Cope (Baton Rouge)

Band 1 Hedwig Kiesel: Martin Luther - ein Held John Osbornes. *Luther* - Kontext und historischer Hintergrund. 1986.

Band 2 Monika Hoffarth: Martin Luther King und die amerikanische Rassenfrage. Stereotypenkorrektur und humanitäre Erziehung durch literarische Rezeption. 1990.

Band 3 Peter Erlebach / Thomas Michael Stein (eds.): Graham Greene in Perspective. A Critical Symposium. 1992.

Band 4 Kevin L. Cope (Ed.): Compendious Conversations. The Method of Dialogue in the Early Enlightenment. 1992.

Band 5 Zaixin Zhang: Voices of the Self in Daniel Defoe's Fiction. An Alternative Marxist Approach. 1993.

Band 6 Berthold Schoene: The Making of Orcadia. Narrative Identity in the Prose Work of George Mackay Brown. 1995.

Band 7 Wolfgang Gehring: Schülernahe Lebensbereiche in Englischbüchern für die 7. Jahrgangsstufe. Ein Beitrag zur landeskundlichen Lehrwerkkritik. 1996.

Band 8 Klaus Stierstorfer: John Oxenford (1812-1877) as Farceur and Critic of Comedy. 1996.

Band 9 Beth Swan: Fictions of Law. An Investigation of the Law in Eighteenth-Century English Fiction. 1997.

Band 10 Catharina Boerckel: Weibliche Entwicklungsprozesse bei Jane Austen, Elizabeth Gaskell und George Eliot. 1997.

Band 11 Rosamaria Loretelli / Roberto De Romanis (Eds.): Narrating Transgression. Representations of the Criminal in Early Modern England. 1999.

Band 12 Nic Panagopoulos: The Fiction of Joseph Conrad. The Influence of Schopenhauer and Nietzsche. 1998.

Band 13 Roland Kofer: Historische Mehrdimensionalität in den Dramen Christopher Frys. Eine hermeneutische Analyse der thematischen Struktur der einzelnen Dramen. 1999.

Band 14 Anke S. Herling: Phantastische Elemente im postmodernen Roman. Formen und Funktionen non-mimetischer Darstellungsweisen in ausgewählten Werken der englischsprachigen Literatur. 1999.

Band 15 Christian J. Ganter: Hoffnung wider die Hoffnungslosigkeit – Das Irlandbild im Erzählwerk Bernard MacLavertys. Ein imagologischer Beitrag zur englischen Literaturdidaktik. 1999.

Band 16 Claudia Oražem: Political Economy and Fiction in the Early Works of Harriet Martineau. 1999.

Band 17 Kwok-kan Tam / Andrew Parkin / Terry Siu-han Yip (eds.): Shakespeare Global / Local. The Hong Kong Imaginary in Transcultural Production. 2002.

Band 18 Matthias Merkl: Kulturgeographische Inhalte in deutschen Lehrbüchern für den Englischunterricht der 8. Jahrgangsstufe. Ein Beitrag zur landeskundlichen Lehrwerkkritik. 2002.

Band 19 Martina Engel: Außenseiter und Gemeinschaft. Zur Funktion von Interaktion, Kommunikation und sozialem Handeln in den Romanen George Eliots. 2002.

Band 20 Bárbara Arizti: *Textuality as Striptease*: The Discourses of Intimacy in David Lodge's *Changing Places* and *Small World*. 2002.

Band 21 Andrew Parkin: The Rendez-Vous. Poems of Multicultural Experience. 2003.

Band 22 Götz Ahrendt: *For our father's sake, and mother's care*. Zur Eltern-Kind-Beziehung in den Dramen Shakespeares unter Berücksichtigung zeitgenössischer Traktatliteratur und Porträts. 2003.

Band 23 Brian Hooper: Voices in the Heart. Postcolonialism and Identity in Hong Kong Literature. 2003.

Band 24 Alexander Bidell: Das Konzept des Bösen in *Paradise Lost*. Analyse und Interpretation. 2003.

Band 25 Isolde Schmidt: Skaespeare im Leistungskurs Englisch. Eine empirische Untersuchung. 2004.

Band 26 Claudia Schemberg: Achieving 'At-one-ment'. Storytelling and the Concept of the *Self* in Ian McEwan's *The Child in Time, Black Dogs, Enduring Love,* and *Atonement.* 2004.

www.peterlang.de